50 AMERICAN HEROES

Every Kid Should Meet!

50
AMERICAN HEROES
Every Kid Should Meet!

by Dennis Denenberg
and Lorraine Roscoe

The Millbrook Press • Brookfield, Connecticut

Acknowledgments

Thank-you to the people who helped
bring this book to fruition:

Byron Hollinshead
Elizabeth McPike
Dr. Harold Robles

Thank-you to the people who
aided our research process:

Kevin Williams
David Dodson
Diana and Don Durand
Richard Yednock
Susan Miller
Charlie Welch
Stephan Williams
Julianne Dickson
Helene Guilfoy
Jane Addams Hull House Association
Stephen Miller, DDS
George C. Marshall Foundation
Helen Keller National Center (HKNC) for
    Deaf-Blind Youth and Adults
Jackie Joyner-Kersee Foundation
Supreme Court of the United States, Public
    Information Office
The dedicated librarians at Millersville University's
    Ganser Library and the Lancaster County Library

Thanks also to Michael G. Roscoe, Allison and
Bethany Roscoe for their continuing patience
and support.

And a special thank-you to Angie Post-Speitel for
crusading to include her hero, Mary McLeod-
Bethune, in this book.

*To my wonderful family and friends,
all of whom have enriched my life.—DD*

*To my mother, whose courage and
indomitable spirit live on. —LR*

Library of Congress Cataloging-in-Publication Data
Denenberg, Dennis, 1947-
50 American heroes every kid should meet /
by Dennis Denenberg and Lorraine Roscoe.
    p. cm.
Includes bibliographical references and index.
ISBN 0-7613-1612-4 (lib. bdg.)
ISBN 0-7613-1645-0 (pbk.)
1. Heroes—United States—Biography—Juvenile
literature. 2. United States—Biography—Juvenile
literature. I. Title: Fifty American heroes every kid
should meet. II. Roscoe, Lorraine, 1955– III. Title.
CT217.D46   2001   920.073—dc21   00-020301

Published by The Millbrook Press, Inc.
2 Old New Milford Road
Brookfield, Connecticut 06804
www.millbrookpress.com

CONTENTS

GEORGE C. MARSHALL
74

ROY ROGERS AND
DALE EVANS
90

JOHN MUIR
76

ELEANOR ROOSEVELT
92

SANDRA DAY O'CONNOR
78

FRANKLIN D. ROOSEVELT
94

ROSA PARKS
80

THEODORE ROOSEVELT
96

I. M. PEI
82

JONAS SALK
98

CHRISTOPHER REEVE
84

TECUMSEH
100

CAL RIPKEN JR.
86

HARRY S TRUMAN
102

JACKIE ROBINSON
AND BRANCH RICKEY
88

HARRIET TUBMAN
104

FOREWORD
by Joy Hakim

The best books tell stories. And I can't imagine a better story than ours—the tale of the United States of America—and of the diverse human beings who came together on this great land and worked and struggled and made us a nation. They did something that was astonishing. They formed a people's nation and founded it on a promise of fairness: liberty and justice for all. Then, so there would be no question about it, they set those goals in writing. No nation anywhere else, of which we knew, had ever done that before.

It wasn't easy. Like all adventures, it demanded heroes—men and women and boys and girls—who accomplished things, who made the nation better for their presence. Once the nation got going, more and different heroes appeared (along with a few villains who had to be thwarted).

So when I heard that Dennis and Lorraine were writing a book about American heroes, I cheered. I knew it was something I would want to read, and I think you will,

too. The 50 heroes in this book include founders, teachers, artists, scientists, world leaders, and some people who might fit right in your neighborhood. You don't have to be a big star to be a hero. Real heroes are often those who quietly do what is right—especially when everyone else seems to be doing something else. You'll be inspired by the people and stories included in this book; you'll learn some things; and you'll have a good time reading, too.

Who are the heroes in your life? Have you ever thought about that? Almost every family has someone heroic—someone who does the right thing when it's important. So does every town. Look around and see if you can discover the heroes in your world. At the same time, maybe you can consider how you might conduct your life so that someday someone writing a book about heroes will include you in it.

Joy Hakim
Author of *A History of US*

INTRODUCTION

READ THIS FIRST!

How quickly can you name 50 American heroes? They can be men or women, young or old, from the past or present, living or dead. But they *all* must have made an exceptional positive contribution to our world.

How'd you do? Were you able to come up with 50 names? Who's on your list? Chances are, a few names popped right up: George Washington, Abraham Lincoln, Dr. Martin Luther King Jr. After all, they have their own national holidays. Then maybe you mentioned people you're studying in school, like Thomas Jefferson, Eleanor Roosevelt, or Charles Lindbergh. After that, perhaps you listed a few important people in the news—Bill Gates, General Colin Powell, maybe even Oprah Winfrey. But you *still* didn't have 50 names, so you moved on to sports stars, rock singers, and other celebrities who may or may not deserve to be heroes. Maybe you even filled out your list with imaginary heroes, like your favorite TV or movie characters.

Coming up with a list of 50 wasn't easy, was it?

We didn't think so either, and that's why we wrote this book. Every kid needs great men and women to admire and imitate, but how can you look up to them if you don't know who they are?

Among our 50 heroes are artists and aviators, activists and scientists, journalists and jurists. They are teachers, musicians, inventors, and athletes. Some are well known; others *deserve* to be. Some of our heroes lived long ago; others continue to enrich our world today. Our heroes share admirable qualities: exceptional talent, fierce determination, and indomitable spirit. They are courageous and confident, and possess an unwavering commitment to being the very best they can be.

And every one is a citizen of the United States.

Can only an American be a hero? Of course not. But America is like no other place in the world. Here, heroes can be rich or poor, male or female, young or old, and of any race, religion, or national origin under the sun. The opportunities open to us are almost endless. We're free to follow any dream that enters our heads, and we have every right to expect fair treatment from others as we do so. It's as simple as that.

So what do these 50 American heroes have to do with you? Everything. They might be what you want to be when you grow up. Although their shoes may seem impossible to fill, you'll find that many of our heroes were a lot like you when they were young. They had families, homes, classmates, part-time jobs. Many had doubts about their own abilities to make a difference in the world.

Read about them. Hear their stories. We've given you a few good books to get you started on finding out more about each of our heroes. Heroes usually seem larger than life. They are so great as to seem almost unreal to us. But all of them are *real* people. Reading their biographies can help you learn more about their childhoods, their friends and families, their hobbies, and all the other ordinary things that make them just like you.

We've also included a number of activities designed to add a little action to your search for heroes. We have given you lots of places—museums, foundations, government agencies—to write to or e-mail. Web site addresses are listed, too, or you can just surf the Net and check out the always-growing list of links to your favorite heroes.

You'll have a great time exploring new ideas, and you won't be alone. As you explore this book, you'll see that we've made it possible for you to interact with us, the authors.

Are our 50 heroes the *only* ones you need to know about? No way! We can name hundreds more men and women who have done great things in their lifetimes. In fact, we want you to find more heroes through our Hero Hunt. Before the Index, on pages 115 to 117, we'll give you clues about men and women similar to the featured heroes. It's up to you to solve the mysteries of who they are. The answers are listed on page 127, but please, NO PEEKING until you have done some digging!

If you believe that some of *your* heroes should have made our list of 50, we'd like to hear from you. Perhaps you know of an accomplished ballet dancer, a brilliant scientist, or a courageous humanitarian that was not on our roster of heroes. Or maybe you admire your grandfather, your teacher, or even an exceptional member of your church, synagogue, mosque, or other place of worship. Contact us and tell us why you hold him or her in such high regard. Better yet, tell your *friends* who your heroes are. The people you look up to can change other kids' lives too, if you're willing to spread the word.

Here's our address:
Heroes4US
P.O. Box 5269
Lancaster, PA 17606-5269

e-mail address:
HEROES4US@aol.com

Visit our Web site:
heroes4us.com

It's time for real heroes.

NOW, MEET THE HEROES. . . .

JANE ADDAMS

September 6, 1860–May 21, 1935

THE FIRST LADY OF PEACE

- **Humanitarian**
- **Author**
- **Recipient, Nobel Peace Prize**

Y ou've probably heard of Mother Teresa, the Roman Catholic nun who devoted her life to helping the world's poor people. But did you know that more than one hundred years ago, an American-born woman did the same? Her name was Jane Addams, and she almost always knew that she wanted to help people.

Jane Addams was a woman of action! While visiting in Europe, she learned of a program in which educated young men moved into a poor section of London and offered classes and activities to people right there in the neighborhood. She thought it was such a great idea that she brought it home and founded Hull House in the slums of Chicago.

Jane Addams shares the fortieth anniversary celebration of Hull House with one of its young residents. Among the reforms benefiting children with which she was associated were the first state child-labor law and the first juvenile court.

In a huge mansion, surrounded by the crowded homes of poor immigrants, Jane Addams and her friends created a haven. There, they taught their neighbors job skills, cared for their children, started a kindergarten, and formed a boys' club (which called itself the Young Heroes Club). Food, friendship, financial help—you could find them all at Hull House.

Jane Addams saw it all very simply: neighbors helping neighbors.

Founded in 1889 in an old mansion, Hull House by 1907 had grown to cover an entire city block. It was torn down in 1963, except for the original mansion and dining hall, which is now a museum. The Hull House Association still provides social services through numerous community centers in Chicago.

"Action is indeed the sole medium of expression for ethics." ("Ethics" is knowing right from wrong.)
—Jane Addams

This group of young boys could be anywhere anytime—but this is 1937, and the game of table hockey is taking place in an alley between two of the Hull House buildings. Always aware of children's recreational needs, Jane Addams and the residents of Hull House organized the first public playground in Chicago in 1893.

In 1979, Mother Teresa (an honorary American citizen) won the Nobel Peace Prize. She followed in the footsteps of the first woman ever to be awarded that prize—Jane Addams.

EXPLORE!

Another cause that got Jane Addams's energy moving and called her to action was world peace. She was the founder and first president of the Women's International League for Peace and Freedom (WIL). Just as she worked hard at Hull House to help the poor, she worked hard to promote world harmony.

Because Jane also wrote numerous books, the WIL has set up an award to honor children's books that promote peace and social justice. We think you will find these books to be great reading. Some of the award-winning books are biographies of heroes, some are stories of young people struggling for freedom, and many are stories of incredible courage. If you would like to read about the events and people who stand for the same values of peace and community that Jane Addams stood for, you can find these books at: www.storyhouse.com (click on *Award Winners*), or by writing to

the Story House Corporation, 1 Bindery Lane, Charlotteville, NY 12036.

EXPLORE SOME MORE!

Does Hull House still exist? Find out by looking up the

Jane Addams Hull House Association
10 South Riverside Plaza
Suite 1700
Chicago, IL 60606
Phone: (800) 448-0083

DIVE IN!

Peace and Bread: The Story of Jane Addams by Stephanie Sammartino McPherson (Carolrhoda Books, 1993), 96 pages. *Trailblazers*

SUSAN B. ANTHONY

February 15, 1820–March 13, 1906

CHAMPION FOR WOMEN'S RIGHTS

- **Suffragette (a woman who advocates the right to vote for women)**
- **Visionary**

Men and Boys Only. No Females Allowed. *Can you imagine that sign being posted at your favorite store? Your favorite fast-food restaurant? How would it make you feel? Now imagine that sign on college applications, on certain careers like medicine and the law. ON VOTING BOOTHS!*

At one time, American women didn't have to imagine any of this. For them, it was real. They were not allowed to do a lot of things that men were allowed to do. And sometimes, they could even be arrested for trying.

In 1869, Susan B. Anthony (*right*) and her friend and fellow women's rights leader, Elizabeth Cady Stanton, founded the National Woman Suffrage Association to work for a woman suffrage amendment to the Constitution. The two women also coedited three volumes of a book called *History of Woman Suffrage*.

On November 5, 1872, Susan B. Anthony broke the law. So did fifteen other women. Eventually, they were all placed under arrest, as were the three men who had allowed them to break the law. The scandal made headlines in newspapers across the country.

What horrible crime had Susan B. Anthony committed? She and fifteen of her friends had voted. They just walked into a polling place and cast their ballots—and in most places in the United States that was against the law.

In the trial that followed many months later, the judge made a mockery of justice. Anthony was the only one of the sixteen women put on trial, and the judge found her guilty and fined her $100 (she never paid it). The three men who let her vote were also found guilty and spent five days in jail.

All this because a woman *voted*!

What did the whole incident prove? Sadly, it showed how women were treated like second-class citizens. Susan B. Anthony couldn't vote, or receive a fair trial. Many of the men in our country wanted to keep all the power and not share it with women.

Unfortunately, she didn't live to see her dream fulfilled, but many of her fellow suffragettes did. In August 1920, the Nineteenth Amendment to the U.S. Constitution was ratified, and women became first-class citizens. They were guaranteed the right to vote. Finally, women were among "we, the people," allowed to take an active part in our democracy.

16

Thanks to the years of work of Susan B. Anthony, all females can cast a ballot when they reach eighteen. Don't take it for granted.

EXPLORE!

Seneca Falls, New York, is the home of the Women's Hall of Fame. Contact:

**The National Women's
Hall of Fame**
76 Fall Street
Seneca Falls, NY 13148
Phone: (315) 568-8060

You'll learn:

- why it's located in Seneca Falls
- who, besides Susan B. Anthony, were the other famous female suffragettes
- what actions they took to get the vote for women

What about the other people in the Hall of Fame? In the introduction to this book, we asked you to help us come up with the next list of 50 heroes. Now's your chance! Find out about the other women and what they did to qualify for this great honor. The Hall of Fame will send you a list of the women and tell you a bit about them. Choose someone who has interests similar to yours and read her biography. Did we include her in this book? Does she belong in the next one? State your case!

Susan B. Anthony came from a Quaker heritage that believed in the equality of men and women—but most Americans, especially men, were not so liberal minded. Many objected to women's involvement in reform movements such as antislavery and temperance—and they particularly objected to giving women the right to vote!

"It was we, the people; not we, the white male citizens; nor yet we, the male citizens; but we, the whole people, who formed the Union."
—Susan B. Anthony

Okay, guys, maybe you're saying "What about a Hall of Fame for men?" Good question. Should we start one? Where would it be? Who should be in it? There are many sports halls of fame (football, baseball, golf, basketball). But what about a Hall of Fame for great men in any field? Should the Women's Hall of Fame be open to men? Is admittance to a Hall of Fame based on gender a sexist idea in itself? Good topic for an essay!

DIVE IN!

Susan B. Anthony: Voice for Women's Voting Rights by Martha E. Kendall (Enslow Publishers, Inc., 1997), 128 pages.
Historical American Biographies

17

CLARA BARTON

Dec. 25, 1821–April 12, 1912

"ANGEL OF THE BATTLEFIELD"

- **Nurse**
- **Humanitarian**
- **Founder, American Red Cross**

September 17, 1862, has been called the bloodiest day of the American Civil War.

It was the day of the Battle of Antietam (some call it the Battle of Sharpsburg), and Clara Barton was there to help care for the wounded. As cannon shells exploded and male nurses ran for cover, she stayed by the surgeon's side, steadying the crude operating table. He later called her "the true heroine of the age, the angel of the battlefield."

She knew she had to go. America's worst flood disaster ever had devastated Johnstown, Pennsylvania. A man-made dam had burst, sending a raging river into the mining town. In just four hours, floodwaters had killed more than two thousand people. Those left behind needed help. They needed Clara Barton and her organization, the American Red Cross.

The year was 1889. Clara spent four months in Johnstown helping the survivors, never once leaving the scene, even for a day. Working from giant tents, she directed hundreds of volunteers in distributing blankets, food, clothes, and money. Flying above her command tent was the red-and-white flag that is now recognized everywhere in America and around the world—the Red Cross flag.

But before the guiding force behind that flag became so famous, she was a shy, withdrawn little girl from a small town in Massachusetts. Clara had always loved helping people. When she was eleven, her brother David fell from a barn roof and was badly hurt. Young Clara would be his nurse. During the next two years, Clara left his bedside for only one-half hour a day!

Nearly thirty years later, Clara Barton would spend day and night caring for the wounded and dying men of the Union army during America's Civil War. She offered her tender care to everyone—Northern soldiers, Southern prisoners of war, white men, and black men.

While recuperating in Switzerland from her American Civil War work, Clara Barton participated in International Committee of the Red Cross activities during the Franco-Prussian War. She is shown here entering Strasbourg with the German army, wearing the Red Cross insignia she was later to make famous in America.

DIVE IN!

Clara Barton: Civil War Nurse
by Nancy Whitelaw
(Enslow Publishers, 1997), 128 pages
Historical American Biographies

18

"[I pledge] before God all that I have, all that I am, all that I can, and all that I hope to be, to the cause of justice and mercy, and patriotism, my country and my God."
—Clara Barton

Clara Barton (front center in dark dress) was the commencement speaker for this 1902 class of graduating nurses. Ms. Barton, of course, did not have the opportunity for formal medical studies when she was young, as it was her groundbreaking work that made modern nursing a real profession.

After the war, she headed the government's search for missing soldiers. She became one of America's most beloved heroes. For the remainder of her life after the Civil War, she continued her humanitarian work and built the organization we know today as the American Red Cross.

EXPLORE!

Its headquarters is a stone's throw from the White House in Washington, D.C. Clara Barton's Red Cross building stands as a sturdy symbol of the organization's commitment to lend a hand whenever and wherever disaster strikes. In the midst of earthquakes, floods, fires, tornadoes, volcanic eruptions, hurricanes, or any other catastrophe, Red Cross volunteers are always there to help. Why? Because they have the same caring spirit as Clara Barton. One of America's strengths has always been its people's willingness to help those whose lives are shattered by disaster.

What about you? Do you want to pitch in? Call your local Red Cross office (the number is in your phone book) or contact the national office of the

American Red Cross
430 17th Street
Washington, DC 20006
On the Web: www.redcross.org

Ask what kinds of things kids your age are doing to help out. Volunteering is the best gift you can offer your community, and it makes you feel pretty good inside, too.

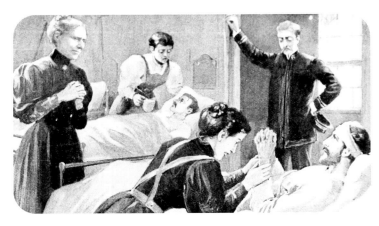

Clara Barton is shown here in Cuba where she supervised nurses after the 1898 explosion of the United States battleship *Maine* in Havana Harbor. Barton's nursing and administrative skills caused her to be present during many famous events in American history, among them the Johnstown, Pennsylvania, flood.

MARY McLEOD BETHUNE

July 10, 1875–May 18, 1955

"THE FIRST LADY OF THE STRUGGLE"

- **Educator**
- **Humanitarian**
- **Civil Rights Activist**

This oil painting hanging in Washington, D.C.'s National Portrait Gallery of the Smithsonian Institution honors Mary McLeod Bethune's many accomplishments, among them being the first black woman to head a federal agency. An appointee of President Franklin D. Roosevelt, she served as director of the Division of Negro Affairs of the National Youth Administration from 1936 to 1944.

More than anything, Mary McLeod Bethune knew that education gives you the power to change your life. Why? Because the opportunity to go to school changed hers.

In Maysville, South Carolina, Mary began her formal education when she was eleven years old. She was the fifteenth of seventeen children of former slaves. Many of her older brothers and sisters had also been born into slavery. Like them, she worked as a child in the cotton fields on her parents' homestead. But something deep inside of Mary—a passion, a spirit, a *hunger* drove her to look for more. Mary wanted to learn and teach and lead. So, in a one-room schoolhouse, with Emma Jane Wilson as her teacher, Mary's new life began.

It's not surprising then that Mary felt so strongly about "giving back" the gift of learning. In 1904, with only $1.50, she opened the Daytona (Florida) Literary and Industrial School for Training Negro Girls. There were only six students (five girls and Mary's son) in this elementary school, but over the next twenty-five years, it grew steadily, transforming into a high school, junior college, and finally Bethune-Cookman College. The story of its survival and growth will forever be the greatest tribute to Mary's determination and energy.

She channeled her energy into other efforts, too. She started a hospital for black people when she saw how discrimination

DIVE IN!

Mary McLeod Bethune: Educator by Malu Halasa (Chelsea House Publishers, 1993), 111 pages. *Black Americans of Achievement*

prevented proper medical care. She became a national spokesperson for the rights of African-Americans prior to our country's dramatic civil-rights movement. She even faced eighty white-hooded Ku Klux Klansmen and forced them to retreat over the issue of blacks having the right to vote. For more than twenty-five years, this human dynamo moved forward with determination, educating, organizing, even advising presidents. She encouraged African Americans, particularly women, to step forward with confidence and dignity and make their voices heard.

EXPLORE!

Over the entrance to one of Bethune-Cookman College's main buildings are the words "Enter to Learn." As you leave the building through these doors, you see the words, "Depart to Serve."

She saw her legacy as reaching far beyond the walls of her college or the organizations that she had founded. She wanted to leave the "principles and policies" in which she firmly believed. "I will pass them on to Negroes everywhere," she wrote, "in the hope that an old woman's philosophy may give them inspiration."

Read Mary's Last Will and Testament. Her words will inspire and make you think. They will encourage you, and show you how proud she was to be an African American. You can find this document on the Internet at: www.nps.gov/mamc/bethune/meet/frame.htm. Read it and think about it. What do her words mean to you today, as a young person? Make a copy of the document and put it away, then take it out in five years. In ten years. In twenty-five years. See if its meaning for you changes as you get older.

An advisor on black affairs to four presidents, Mary McLeod Bethune (second from left) proudly looks on as President Harry S Truman signs a bill proclaiming February 1 as National Freedom Day. This special day commemorates the signing of the Constitution's Thirteenth Amendment, which banned slavery.

"I leave you love . . . I leave you hope . . . I leave you the challenge of developing confidence in one another . . . I leave you a thirst for education . . . I leave you respect for the uses of power . . . I leave you faith . . . I leave you racial dignity . . . I leave you a desire to live harmoniously with your fellow men . . . I leave you finally a responsibility to our young people."

—from the Last Will and Testament of Mary McLeod Bethune

EXPLORE SOME MORE!

There's a great statue of Mary McLeod Bethune in Washington, D.C. It's the first statue placed to honor an African-American woman in the United States. Find a picture of it in a book or on the Internet. Go see it if you can!

21

ELIZABETH BLACKWELL

February 3, 1821–May 31, 1910

FIRST AMERICAN WOMAN DOCTOR

- **Physician**
- **Humanitarian**
- **Trailblazer**

There's nothing unusual about a female doctor. But not so long ago, a lot of people thought the idea was ridiculous.

Even when she was young, Elizabeth Blackwell was strong-willed and stubborn, not reserved and submissive like girls were expected to be.

But not even young Elizabeth considered studying medicine. Not until a dying friend planted the seed. Her sick neighbor appreciated the hours that Elizabeth spent taking care of her. "If I could have been treated by a lady doctor, my worst sufferings would have been spared me," she said. "If only *you* were a doctor."

Elizabeth a doctor? Well, why not? It was a path no woman had ever attempted to follow. Medical schools were for men only, so Elizabeth Blackwell spent years preparing with the help of some friendly doctors before she even applied. She wanted to be ready to succeed.

She was twenty-five when she began to apply to medical schools. She collected rejection after rejection—from all of them.

DIVE IN!

Elizabeth Blackwell: A Doctor's Triumph
by Nancy Kline and Nancy Neveloff Dubler
(Conari Press, 1997), 208 pages.
Barnard Biography, Vol. 2

Although her fellow medical students voted her into the school as a joke, Blackwell earned their respect. Her only real problem was being the only female in the class on human reproduction. She later recalled: "Some of the students blushed, some were hysterical . . . I had to pinch my hand till the blood nearly came . . . to keep me from smiling."

More rejection letters came, bringing the total to twenty-eight. How would you feel? Would you give up?

Then, the letter from Geneva Medical College in New York arrived. *Acceptance!* She was finally on the road to earning her medical degree. Only upon arriving at the college did she learn why she was accepted. It was a joke! The school's faculty had not wanted her, but in order to avoid making that decision, they asked the all-male student body to vote. The men voted unanimously for her entry. They figured some other medical school was playing a practical joke. But the joke was on them. The Geneva faculty had to honor the vote, and Elizabeth Blackwell was in.

And she had the last laugh. After the two-year program was over, Dr. Elizabeth Blackwell graduated number one in her class. The struggle had been long and lonely, but she made it. She was a doctor.

However, Dr. Blackwell did not then coast on to fame and fortune. After all, she had to convince patients to allow themselves to be *examined* by a female doctor! What followed was a roller-coaster life of accomplishment and disappointment. She would need every ounce of her intelligence, determination, and independent spirit to make it work. Do you think she did it? Do you think we would have included her in this book if she didn't?

EXPLORE!

Dr. Blackwell dedicated her life to curing people. How much do you know about first aid? Could you help a friend who suddenly was injured? Would you know what simple things to do and not to do? You can be ready to help a family member or friend by learning CPR, mouth-to-mouth resuscitation, the Heimlich maneuver, and other first-aid techniques. By staying calm and acting responsibly, you might be able to save a life until the 911 emergency squad arrives.

How do you get this information? First, check with your school nurse, who can probably give you a pamphlet on first aid. The American Red Cross, scouting groups, and youth organizations all provide training. The Web site for the American Red Cross is: www.redcross.org. This informative site will pinpoint the Red Cross instruction location closest to your home.

Hobart and William Smith Colleges now consider Blackwell among their most distinguished alumnae, evidenced by this 800-pound, larger-than-life bronze sculpture that sits near one of the colleges' most traveled walkways. Sculptor Professor A. E. Ted Aub worked from the few available photographs of Blackwell as well as her diaries in order to render her as she might have looked in her student days.

POWER WORDS

"For what is done or learned by one class of women becomes, by virtue of their common womanhood, the property of all women."
—Elizabeth Blackwell

RACHEL CARSON

May 27, 1907–April 14, 1964

"A SOLITARY CHILD"

- **Environmentalist**
- **Author**

Rachel Carson's love of books and animals shone through at an early age. Here she is shown reading aloud to her dog, Candy.

Rachel Carson called herself "a solitary child." She loved to spend "a great deal of time in woods and beside streams, learning the birds and the insects and flowers." Being out in nature made her feel good about herself. She also fell in love with reading and writing when she was very young. Those interests—nature, reading, and writing—would one day make young Rachel Carson a famous crusader.

St. Nicholas was a magazine for kids. In fact, it was the most popular children's magazine when Rachel Carson was a ten-year-old growing up in Springdale, Pennsylvania. This magazine asked its readers to submit poems, stories, and drawings for publication. If you got published, you got *paid*. When she was ten, Rachel sold a story, to *St. Nicholas*, and they paid her ten dollars. This was the beginning of Rachel's professional writing career.

Later in life, Rachel Carson would combine her love of nature with her love and talent for writing. Mostly she wrote about ecology, conservation, and the environment. These are things we talk about all the time, but in her day, people thought only scientists needed to know about such things. They didn't realize how precious our environment is, and how we have to work together to protect it.

Rachel Carson helped change all that. She was a courageous as well as a talented writer. In her last book, *Silent Spring*, she challenged many wealthy and influential people in business and government by telling the world how the use of pesticides was poisoning the planet. Her opponents ridiculed her, but others listened and learned. Thanks to her brave words, the food we eat is no longer contaminated with the dangerous pesticide called DDT.

EXPLORE!

"Freedom of the press" is guaranteed under our Bill of Rights (the U.S. Constitution's first ten amendments). It means that writers can write about almost anything, as long as they tell the truth.

Rachel Carson saw a wrong and tried to right it by using the power of the freedom of the press in writing about it. You can do the same! Maybe there's a dangerous intersection in your town or neighborhood that needs a traffic light or stop sign to be made safe. Maybe classrooms in your school are overcrowded. Maybe you know about a

"In nature, nothing exists alone."
—from *Silent Spring*
by Rachel Carson

place where people are dumping trash illegally. Use the "power of the pen" to try and change things.

Write letters to the editor of your local newspaper, write to the mayor and town council, write to a particular business or company—write to the people who can change the things you know are bad and should be changed. *Offer solutions* to the problem when you write about it, just as Rachel Carson did when she wrote that the solution to pesticide pollution was to stop using them.

EXPLORE SOME MORE!

Contact the **Rachel Carson Council, Inc.,** for more information on current efforts to fight toxic and chemical threats to our environment. The address is 8940 Jones Mill Road, Chevy Chase, MD 20815. Phone: (301) 652-1877. They are also on the Web.

Some other organizations concerned with preserving our planet are:

National Wildlife Federation
1412 16th Street NW
Washington, DC 20036

Citizens for a Better Environment
407 South Dearborn
Suite 1775
Chicago, IL 60605

Surf the Net and see if you can find these organizations and others.

DIVE IN!

Rachel Carson by Judith J. Presnall (Lucent Books, 1995), 96 pages.

Rachel Carson by Jake Goldberg (Chelsea House Publishers, 1991), 76 pages. *Junior World Biographies*

Also, please read *Silent Spring* (Houghton Mifflin, 1962). Then you'll see firsthand how powerful Rachel Carson's words really are.

The Rachel Carson Refuge in Wells, Maine, is part of a wetland acquisition program to preserve valuable wildlife habitats at key locations along waterfowl migration routes. When completed, it will consist of 7,435 acres of salt marsh and adjacent freshwater habitats. More than 250 species of birds can be observed on or from the refuge during the year.

JIMMY CARTER

October 1, 1924–

PEACEMAKER

- **U.S. President**
- **Humanitarian**
- **Public Servant**

Only in America could a peanut farmer named Jimmy become president of the United States and remain a statesman respected around the world.

Camp David is our presidents' vacation home. In 1978, President Jimmy Carter brought two extraordinary world leaders to Camp David: Anwar Sadat, the president of Egypt, and Menachem Begin, the prime minister of Israel. These two Middle Eastern countries had been at war for more than thirty years. Many people, including children, had been killed in battle and by acts of terrorism. The two nations had very different views. But Jimmy Carter believed that if he could get Sadat and Begin to talk face-to-face, they could begin to work out their problems. It was a bold move for peace. And it worked!

Amazingly, one of the simple things our president did that kept the peace talks going was to autograph some photos. The Israeli leader had requested autographed pictures of the three men together. He wanted them for his grandchildren. Well, President Carter had his secretary find out the names of these special kids and he personalized each photo. When Begin was handed the pictures, he politely thanked the president. Then he looked at the autographs

One of Jimmy Carter's major activities is working on behalf of Habitat for Humanity, an organization that builds simple, affordable houses in partnership with those in need of adequate shelter. With the help of volunteers, Habitat has built more than 30,000 houses across the United States since 1976. Kids can also help, so look into it at http://www.habitat.org/how/tour /1.html.

The agreement signed by Anwar Sadat, Menachem Begin, and Jimmy Carter is known as the "Camp David Accords." Thanks to President Carter's creative efforts, the Middle East became a safer and more peaceful place—at least temporarily.

and read their names. His grandchildren's names. Suddenly, the tough old leader's eyes filled with tears. The sight of those names led him to talk about those special people in his life, and about the terrible effects of war on children. Dramatically, the tone of the talks turned around—and a settlement was reached.

EXPLORE!

President Carter lost his reelection campaign in 1980. Sometimes, ex-presidents don't quite know what to do, but not Jimmy Carter. He has been one of our busiest former chief executives. And he has become one of the most respected and recognized Americans in the world. That's because he has devoted his time and energy to peace-making missions around the globe. Some of the places he's been to may be familiar to you. Others probably are not. He's been all over the planet working for peace, human rights, and democracy—in Bosnia, Panama, Nicaragua, Haiti, Ethiopia, North and South Korea, and, of course, in the Middle East.

You can find out about these efforts and what Jimmy Carter is currently doing by contacting the **Carter Center** in Atlanta, Georgia. Contact the Center at

453 Freedom Parkway
Atlanta, GA 30307
Phone: (404) 331-3900
On the Web: www.CarterCenter.org

One of the special projects in progress at the Carter Center is called Global 2000. It involves working to promote democracy by fighting poverty, hunger, and disease. Its work is very practical, not just politicians talking about what to do. For example, there's one research team working to destroy the Guinea worm, a terrible parasite found in African countries and in India. Find out what other things Global 2000 is trying to do, and maybe you can help.

DIVE IN!

Jimmy Carter: On the Road to Peace by Caroline Evenson Lano (Silver Burdett Press, 1996), 160 pages.

Jimmy Carter by Anne E. Schraff (Enslow Publishers, Inc., 1998), 128 pages.

27

GEORGE WASHINGTON CARVER

c. (circa) 1864–January 5, 1943

THE REAL "MR. PEANUT"

- **Educator**
- **Plant Scientist**
- **Agriculture Innovator**

George Washington Carver once told a story about a conversation he had with God. He asked God to tell him the mystery of the universe. God replied that George was asking about something much too grand. Then George asked God to tell him all about the peanut. And God decided that the peanut was much more nearly George's size. So God showed George what the peanut was all about.

Next time you gobble up a peanut butter and jelly sandwich, think of George Washington Carver. He turned the humble peanut into an agricultural giant.

What got him interested in peanuts? It all started with an insect. In the late 1800s, cotton was the major cash crop for farmers in the Southern states. But the dreaded Mexican boll weevil was threatening to eat the plants and destroy the farmers' income. Besides, all that cotton growing was wearing out the land. The farmers needed a change. Farmers, however, were scared to switch. They knew how to raise cotton, and they knew cotton would sell. Dr. Carver realized that if he were to get farmers to change their habits, he had to prove to them that some other crop would be just as valuable as cotton.

Experimenting, he came up with more than three hundred ways to use peanuts. There were dyes, fruit punches (cherry, lemon, and orange), milk, facial cream, ink, relish, and even a peanut curd that tasted just like meat. Dr. Carver had proven that peanuts had potential.

This great scientist had always been interested in plants and insects even when he was a boy. But learning about the natural world around him was not easy. He was born a slave and battled terrible discrimination against African Americans his entire life. Yet, George Washington Carver was determined to succeed, and succeed he did. He became a gifted and respected botanist. He was invited to be a professor at Tuskegee Institute in Alabama. After his death, the U.S. Congress paid tribute to him by dedicating his birthplace site near Diamond Grove, Missouri, as a national monument.

President Franklin D. Roosevelt said of George Washington Carver: "The things which he achieved in the face of early handicaps will for all time afford an inspiring example to youth everywhere."

DIVE IN!

George Washington Carver: Nature's Trailblazer by Teresa Rogers (Twenty-First Century Books, Inc., 1995), 88 pages. Illustrated. *Earthkeepers*

" . . . it has always been the one great ideal of my life to be of the greatest good to the greatest number of 'my people' possible, and to this end I have been preparing myself for these many years; feeling as I do that this line of education is the key to unlock the golden door of freedom to our people. . . ."
—George Washington Carver

The depth of commitment to his research was made clear when Carver, in the hope of setting an example for others, donated his entire life savings of $33,000 to Tuskegee Institute to establish a fund to carry on the agricultural and chemical work he began.

EXPLORE!

America has often been called "the land of opportunity" because people of any color, religion, or ethnic background can be successful. We are free to follow our dreams, just like the "peanut doctor" did.

Scientists often use their imaginations when they pursue their dreams. They try to come up with new ways to look at concepts, objects, and facts, like Professor Carver did with the peanut. Your task is to take a common natural product (like a potato or a daisy or a dog hair) and become Professor Carver. Design new ways for that product to be used. Consider what you know or can find out about the product, and then let your imagination run wild. If you can, test your new ideas to see if they work. Great things can happen when thinkers like you play with the impossible!

MARY CASSATT

May 22, 1844–January 14, 1926

"AMERICA'S GREAT IMPRESSIONIST"

- **Artist**

Mary Cassatt painted this portrait of herself when she was in her mid-thirties. The original watercolor, cheerful with its bright yellow background, hangs in the National Portrait Gallery in Washington, D.C.

Young women in the nineteenth century simply did not have careers. Their proper place was in the home, as a wife and mother. Certainly, it was acceptable to be talented in the so-called parlor arts like sewing, embroidery, and occasional painting. But pursuing art as a career? Never! Reportedly, Mary Cassatt's father even said, "I would almost rather see you dead."

But Mary Stevenson Cassatt would not be discouraged. Not by her dad, not by her art teachers (who were all men, by the way), not by other artists (who were *also* mostly men). She spent years training and practicing, always eager to learn, improve, and change. She studied and worked in France, Italy, and Spain.

The turning point in her artistic career came when, upon the invitation of a French artist named Edgar Degas, Mary Cassatt was asked to join a group labeled "Impressionists." These rebels in the art world were willing to look for new ways to use

Cassatt's closest friend among the Impressionist painters was Edgar Degas, who strongly influenced her style.

color and light in their paintings, and they wanted to paint subjects that traditional painters never considered. Mary and a growing number of French artists felt that there shouldn't be rules about how you paint. Among this group of artists, Cassatt found her place and, as she later said, "began to live."

Even her father was proud of his daughter's acceptance in the European art world.

EXPLORE!

Read Mary Cassatt's Power Words. Curious, aren't they? This very successful artist was not satisfied with her many achievements.

30

She felt she could have done even more with her life and the legacy of great art she left us.

To appreciate what she did, you need to see her work, preferably in person. So, we want you to be ready when a Mary Cassatt exhibit comes to your area. Keep an eye on your newspaper. If you live close to a major city, contact the art museum there and ask to be notified when a Cassatt exhibit is scheduled. In the meantime, check out her work on the Internet. Just search for "Mary Cassatt" using your favorite search engine.

Also expand your universe by checking out local exhibits, even in your own school. Every spring, Scholastic Inc. sponsors awards programs in art and writing for middle-school and high-school students. Check their Web site.

"I have not yet done what I wanted to, but I tried to make a good fight."

—Mary Cassatt

EXPLORE SOME MORE!

Mary Cassatt and the Impressionists broke the art world's rules when they painted, and our world is richer for it.

In 1978 the late Harry Chapin (a popular story-songwriter), wrote "Flowers Are Red." This song tells of a little boy who, during art class at school, paints a world where not all flowers are red and not all leaves are green. Instead he sees "so many colors in a rainbow . . . the morning sun . . . a flower . . ."

and he wants to use every one! Track down this song—it is in the album *Living Room Suite*, produced in 1978 on the Elektra label. Check with music stores, your local library, and on the Internet. Find out what happens to the little boy. Do his teachers nurture his colorful vision? Or do they squash it?

DIVE IN!

Mary Cassatt: Portrait of an American Expressionist by Thomas Streissguth (Lerner Publishing Group, 1998), 112 pages

Considered radical at the time, scenes of everyday domestic life were favorites with Cassatt. She became well known for her paintings of mothers and children such as this pastel, entitled *In the Garden.*

CESAR CHAVEZ AND DOLORES HUERTA

Chavez: March 31, 1927–April 23, 1993   *Huerta: April 10, 1930–*

CHAMPIONS OF THE MIGRANT WORKERS

- **Labor Leaders**
- **Civil Rights Activists**

Those of you who have moved know that means change. It means giving up some things you like. It means learning and adapting. Now imagine young Cesar's life. By the time he was in the eighth grade, he had attended more than three dozen different schools! Why? Because his family members were migrant workers.

Migrant workers are the hardworking people who harvest many of the fruits and vegetables we eat. While machines can help, men, women, and children still pick the crops. Migrant workers settle wherever there's produce to pick, then move on when the work is done.

Living conditions for migrant farmworkers were awful. In the 1960s they were making a dollar an hour for long workdays. They traveled in rickety trucks and buses to fields sprayed with pesticide poisons. Their homes were crowded, dismal shacks without electricity or running water.

Migrant workers had no money, no power, and no voice. When Cesar grew up, he became their voice, as did Dolores Huerta. Teamwork brought them together, and they started the organization known as the United Farm Workers of America. (UFW). By using labor strikes and boycotts, Cesar Chavez and Dolores Huerta made Americans aware of just how bad conditions were for migrant workers.

Chavez's nonviolent demonstrations eventually resulted in tens of thousands of agricultural workers enjoying higher pay, family health coverage, pension benefits, and other protections that came from working under UFW contracts.

Together they led peaceful protests, made speeches, and started the "Boycott Grapes" campaign. The country paid attention to this team. We stopped eating grapes and drinking wine from non–worker-friendly vineyards. The growers paid attention, and life improved for migrant farmworkers.

32

Dolores Huerta (*left*) joins Ethel Kennedy in prayer for Cesar Chavez outside the Monterey County, California, jail. Chavez was jailed for violating a court injunction prohibiting a boycott of lettuce.

EXPLORE!

Sometimes, if we don't hear anything about a problem for a while, we think it's solved. How about the migrant workers' problems? Has their situation improved? Or is there still work to do?

Do some research. An article by Evelyn Nieves, published in 1996 by *The New York Times* News Service, says little has changed. Find this article and others in the library or on the Internet. What do you think? Is there any way you can help?

If there are children of migrant workers in your school, could you help them adapt to their new class? Perhaps your local place of worship could have a special program to lend a hand to migrant workers in your area.

DIVE IN!

Cesar Chavez: Leader for Migrant Farm Workers by Doreen Gonzales (Enslow Publishers, Inc. 1996), 128 pages.

Dolores Huerta by Frank Perez (Raintree/Steck Vaughn, 1996), 48 pages. *Contemporary Hispanic Americans*

POWER WORDS

"Students must have initiative; they should not be mere imitators. They must learn to think and act for themselves and be free."

—Cesar Chavez

"I would like to be remembered as a woman who cares for fellow humans. We must use our lives to make the world a better place to live, not just to acquire things. That is what we are put on the earth for."

—Dolores Huerta

ROBERTO CLEMENTE

August 18, 1934–December 31, 1972

"AN MVP ON AND OFF THE FIELD"

- **Athlete**
- **Humanitarian**

Four-time Batting Champion, National League

Most Valuable Player (MVP), National League—1966

Twelve-time winner, Golden Glove for Fielding Proficiency

MVP, World Series—1971

Eleventh player to achieve 3,000 hits in his major-league career

Clemente receives a silver bat in honor of his 1965 National League Batting Championship.

s a member of the Pittsburgh Pirates baseball team, Roberto Clemente racked up a list of super statistics. But if that's all you know about him, you don't really know what makes Roberto Clemente a hero. It's more than MVP honors. It's the quality of his life and his giving.

Raised in a loving family, he learned important values as a child that would guide him for the rest of his life. Work hard. Do the very best you can. Be humble. Always care about others.

And Clemente did care about others. For many years, even after becoming one of baseball's great players, he would spend the off-season helping others with his time and energy as well as his money. When a terrible earthquake destroyed much of the city

Always mindful of his young fans, Clemente signs baseballs at the Hiram Bithorn Stadium in San Juan, Puerto Rico.

of Managua in the Central American country of Nicaragua, he wanted to help. He organized relief efforts to take food and medical supplies there. When he heard that supplies were being stolen and weren't reaching those who needed them, he was outraged. He decided to deliver the provisions personally, insisting, "They will not dare to steal from Roberto Clemente."

On New Year's Eve, he boarded a rickety old DC–7 cargo plane and took off on his mission. Moments after takeoff, the plane went down, killing everyone on board. Clemente's body was never found.

Days later, the Baseball Writers of America elected Roberto Clemente to the Hall of Fame, waiving the requirement that a player must be retired for five years. What a tribute to his achievements on and off the playing field.

EXPLORE!

Only a few people can become MVPs in the sports world, but every one of us can be an MVP in life by helping other people like Roberto Clemente did. Read his Power Words. He's telling us to make things better in our world. Kind of makes you feel embarrassed if you don't do something, doesn't it?

We're not necessarily talking about finding a cure for cancer or filling a plane with supplies for the poor. We're talking about the little things you can do every day—at school,

DIVE IN!

Pride of Puerto Rico: The Life of Roberto Clemente by Robert Walker (Harcourt Brace, 1991), 158 pages.

POWER WORDS

"Any time you have the opportunity to accomplish something for somebody who comes behind you and you don't do it, you are wasting your time on this earth."
—Roberto Clemente

at home, with your friends, whatever. For example, when was the last time you did an extra chore at home without being asked? *Without* complaining? Check your conscience. Look around you at school. Any way to make things better there?

What you do to "make things better" is up to you. You might collect food for a food bank . . . teach your little brother how to tie his shoes . . . play checkers with the old man who lives next door . . . empty the dishwasher . . . send a card to your grandmother . . . you figure it out!

Need a little inspiration? Read Clemente's biography, or visit the official Roberto Clemente Web site at: www.robertoclemente21.com. Find out about the Roberto Clemente Foundation, which funds recreational and educational programs for inner-city kids in Pittsburgh. Read about Roberto Clemente Sports City in Puerto Rico, where children play sports and take part in other activities. Make the time. Make the commitment. Make it happen.

BILL COSBY

July 12, 1937–

DR. COSBY

- **Actor**
- **Teacher**
- **Author**
- **Humanitarian**

While *The Cosby Show* debunked racial stereotypes on screen, Cosby used its success to fight behind-the-scenes discrimination within the television industry.

Wait a minute. Isn't Bill Cosby that funny guy on TV? His TV shows and his stand-up comedy routines are funny. So are his books, comedy albums, and cartoon creations. Ever hear of "Hey, hey, hey, it's Fat Albert"? That's a Cosby! But the Bill Cosby who's a hero does more than make us laugh. He's also Dr. William H. Cosby, educator and serious advocate for kids.

Bill grew up in a poor Philadelphia neighborhood. He struggled with school (wasn't very good at it) and doing odd jobs. Then one of those jobs (tending bar) led to his first big break as a comedian. Once he found his talent, Bill was determined to be successful. He was, and with success came a sense of responsibility:

- Responsibility to finish his education. Not only did he complete high school, but he also earned a doctorate in education. He used what he learned to design educational shows for television.

- Responsibility to raise a family, in real life and on television. *The Cosby Show*, about a loving African-American family,

won a mountain of awards and ran for eight seasons. Cosby even wrote a book called *Fatherhood* that sold three million copies!

- Responsibility to help others with the money he made throughout his career. Cosby set up scholarship funds, donates dollars for research to fight diseases, and uses his money to alleviate poverty. He gives back to the community because he remembers the struggles of his childhood.

"The Cos" is that funny guy on TV—with a big heart and a big sense of responsibility. A hero.

DIVE IN!

Bill Cosby: America's Most Famous Father by Jim Haskins (Walker & Co. Library, 1988), 138 pages.

"He was my hero."
—Bill Cosby
(speaking of
his son, Ennis,
who was murdered
at the age of 27)

EXPLORE!

Four simple words spoken by Bill Cosby touched a lot of people in 1997. "He was my hero." Bill wasn't talking about a famous person like a president, a great artist, or a super athlete. He was talking about his son, Ennis, who was shot and killed while changing a tire on a road in California. Bill and his family were devastated by the tragedy.

Ennis was a twenty-seven-year-old student at Columbia University when he died. He had dyslexia, a learning disability, and he wanted to spend his life working with kids with learning disabilities. He dreamed of

Cosby and his wife, Camille, who also has a doctorate, have made significant donations to many African-American organizations, including the National Association for the Advancement of Colored People (NAACP), the United Negro College Fund, the National Sickle-Cell Foundation, and the National Council of Negro Women. In 1989 they gave their biggest gift, of $20 million, to Spelman College.

creating a school for those kids. Then, in an instant, Bill Cosby's son, his hero, was gone.

Now's the time to think about the heroes in your life. It could be anybody you admire. Maybe a parent, a brother, or a sister. Maybe a coach or a teacher or a Scout leader. Maybe it's just a person who spreads encouragement when others need it most. Your hero can help you, teach you, guide you, love you, just like Ennis and his father helped, taught, guided, and loved one another.

Tell your hero that he or she is special to you. Chances are your hero doesn't even know. Send your hero a card. Give him or her a hug. Say "thank you."

Bill Cosby is generous not only with his money but also with his time and effort on behalf of a cause in which he believes. Here he joins a picket line supporting equal opportunity employment.

WALT DISNEY

December 5, 1901–December 15, 1966

THE FIRST IMAGINEER

- **Animator**
- **Filmmaker**
- **Dreamer**

"Disney" is possibly the most recognized name in the world! But how much do you know about the real man named Disney . . . Mickey's dad . . . the man who taught us to "Wish Upon a Star"?

Hardly anyone believed it would work. "The idea is flawed." "People won't pay attention." "It's a waste of time, money, and talent." Not exactly words of encouragement? But Walt Disney believed in the project, and since he was the company's founder and driving force, it was going to happen. His brother, Roy, had learned long before not to try to talk Walt out of something he wanted to do.

This charcoal drawing of Disney flanked by characters of his own creation hangs in the National Portrait Gallery in Washington, D.C.

It took about three years (1934–1937) to finish it, and it cost almost $1.5 million, an enormous amount of money in the midst of the country's Great Depression. But on December 21, 1937, all the doubters and disbelievers had to admit that they were wrong. The project that competitors had labeled "Disney's Folly" was an overnight smash hit, and it changed the world of entertainment forever. What are we talking about? Maybe you've seen it—a little masterpiece

Disney "holds up" a stagecoach full of smiling youngsters in a 1954 photo to publicize Disneyland, his soon-to-be-opened theme park. His parks have been making children smile ever since!

In a charming Academy Award ceremony moment, young Shirley Temple presents Walt Disney one large Oscar and seven little ones for his movie, *Snow White and the Seven Dwarfs.*

"Somehow, I can't believe there are many heights that can't be scaled by a man who knows the secret of making dreams come true."

—Walt Disney

called *Snow White and the Seven Dwarfs,* the very first full-length animated movie ever made.

Today, we can watch full-length feature cartoons with excellent artwork, computer animation, memorable music, and big-name stars supplying voices for the tigers and teapots on the screen. But Walt Disney began this phenomenon with a sketchbook and a dream. His imagination evolved into a new kind of worldwide entertainment.

Walt once said, "It's kind of fun to do the impossible."

DIVE IN!

The Man Behind the Magic: The Story of Walt Disney by Katherine and Richard Greene (Viking Children's Books, 1998), 192 pages.

EXPLORE!

Bet you thought we were going to send you off to Walt Disney World or Disneyland for this one. No such luck!

It's time you know more about the original "Imagineer"—the clever name given to the creative people at the Disney studios. They are **Imagi**native engi**neers**.

Read the biography we suggest in Dive In and get to know the man who made the magic happen. How did he handle failure? What inspired him? What made him laugh? Then we have a major assignment for you. When you visit the amazing theme parks named after Walt, you'll find practically nothing there about this great man. We think everyone who visits Walt Disney World or Disneyland should be able to learn about the "founding father" of it all. So we want you to design something about him for the parks. It could be a new ride or attraction, a souvenir, a . . . well, you tell us. Use your imagination. You can E-mail all of your ideas to the Disney organization by going to: disney.go.com/mail/ and following the directions.

FREDERICK DOUGLASS

February 7, 1817–February 20, 1895

"THE VOICE OF FREEDOM"

- **Abolitionist**
- **Author**
- **Orator**

Right now, you're doing what for Frederick Douglass was an illegal activity that enabled him to become a free man. You are reading.

It was against the law to teach a slave to read and write. If a slave could read, the slave might start to think about ideas like freedom, justice, and fairness. That sounded like trouble to slave owners. But Mrs. Auld didn't know the law when eight-year-old Frederick was given to her family.

Frederick had lots of chores to do in the house, but life at the Auld home in Baltimore was better than he'd ever known—his owner actually taught him to read.

Then Mrs. Auld told her husband of Frederick's rapid progress and his eagerness to read. Mr. Auld had a fit! He knew the law. He knew how important it was to keep slaves from learning to read. He ordered her to stop.

But it was too late. The seeds of Frederick's freedom had been sown. He found other ways to continue to learn. White playmates helped him when they could. The slave owners were right. Reading did teach Frederick about freedom, justice, and fairness. And he wanted some, for himself and for every other slave in the land.

When he was twenty years old, Douglass escaped from slavery. As a free man, he enthusiastically joined the abolitionists—the antislavery activists who were working hard to end the nightmare. He gave powerful speeches describing and denouncing the

Frederick Douglass's life spanned nearly eighty years, from the time that slavery was universal in the American states to the time it was becoming a memory—a change in which he played a major role.

horrors of slavery. He established an antislavery newspaper called *North Star*, and directed a branch of the Underground Railroad, which was the escaped slave's route north to freedom.

At one point, Douglass's opponents tried to use his skills as a writer and orator to discredit him. They insisted that he was too impressive to have been a slave. That's when he wrote his famous autobiography, *The Narrative of the Life of Frederick Douglass: An American Slave.*

Slavery had stolen Frederick Douglass's childhood, destroyed his family, and abused generations of his people. He vowed to see it struck down. And indeed he did. The

Renowned for his eloquence, Douglass lectured throughout the United States and England on the brutality and immorality of slavery. Here he is shown being attacked by an angry mob at an abolitionist meeting in Boston, a year before the Civil War began.

American Civil War was fought, Lincoln issued his Emancipation Proclamation, Congress enacted the Thirteenth Amendment to the Constitution, and slavery was gone. Thanks, in part, to an eight-year-old slave who learned to read.

EXPLORE!

Frederick Douglass was very young when his master's wife turned him on to the power of the written word. Learning to read changed his life, and eventually moved him to try to change the lives of people wrapped in slavery's chains.

So why don't *you* change someone's life? *You* can read, but not everyone can. Many

DIVE IN!

Frederick Douglass: In His Own Words edited by Milton Meltzer (Harcourt, Brace, Jovanovich, 1995), 240 pages.

students struggle with reading every day. Their parents or teachers often don't have time to give them the extra help they need. But *you* have time. Ask your teacher or guidance counselor if there's a tutoring program you can help with. Call your local library and see if they need someone to read to the little kids or help older ones with research projects.

Literacy Volunteers of America, Inc., is a nonprofit organization dedicated to helping adults learn to read. Check out their Web site: www.literacyvolunteers.org. Is there a local chapter in your community? Call the United Way headquarters in your area. They usually have a directory of service groups. Maybe you can join one that helps people learn to read.

Who knows? The person you read with today could become an American hero every kid should meet. Wouldn't it be cool to know that *you* helped make it happen?

POWER WORDS

"No man can put a chain about the ankle of his fellow man without at last finding the other end fastened about his own neck."
—Frederick Douglass

THOMAS ALVA EDISON

February 11, 1847–October 18, 1931

"THE WIZARD OF MENLO PARK"

- **Inventor**
- **Genius**

A patent is a special piece of paper issued by the U.S. government. All you have to do is invent something no one else has, and then you own that invention. The patent paper is proof that you did it. Thomas Alva Edison took out 1,093 patents during his eighty-four years on the planet. If he had invented one new thing each day, that translates into three solid years worth of one-of-a-kind ideas.

During his lifetime, Edison was the most famous American in the world. His inventions include the incandescent light (you call it a lightbulb), the phonograph (great-granddaddy of your CD player), and the motion picture (as in "movie") projector. So much of what we use and enjoy today was born in Thomas Edison's creative mind. He was a genius.

When Tom was a boy, his teachers thought he was stupid because he asked so many questions. But his mom understood his never-ending need to know.

Tom was a genius, but he was also a master of trial and error. If something did not work, Edison always kept trying! He never seemed to get discouraged. He always believed that eventually he would succeed.

If you want to be impressed, go to http://edison.rutgers.edu/patents.htm for a complete descriptive list of all 1,093 successful U.S. patent applications—but keep in mind that Edison filed an estimated 500 to 600 unsuccessful or abandoned applications as well!

When he set out to invent a storage battery, he probably didn't expect it to take 8,001 attempts to find a material that would hold an electrical charge. But when asked about this invention, he replied, "Well, at least we know 8,000 things that *don't* work." Edison proved that success comes to those who never quit.

EXPLORE!

Contact these Edison museums:

The Edison Winter Home and Museum
2350 McGregor Boulevard
Fort Myers, FL 33901
Phone: (914) 334-3614
On the Web: www.edison-ford-estate.com

DIVE IN!

Thomas Alva Edison: Inventing the Electric Age by Gene Adair (Oxford University Press, Inc., 1996), 141 pages.

Thomas Edison Birthplace Museum
9 Edison Drive
Box 451
Milan, OH 44846
Phone: (419) 499-2135

Henry Ford Museum and Greenfield Village
20900 Oakwood Boulevard
Box 1970
Dearborn, MI 48121-1970
Phone: (313) 982-6001 or
(800) 835-5237
On the Web: www.hfmgv.org

Edison National Historical Site
Main Street at Lakeside Avenue
West Orange, NJ 07052
Phone: (201) 736-5050
On the Web: www.nps.gov/edis

They'll send you some cool information about the inventor; maybe you'll even plan a trip to these places.

Now, conduct 9,990 experiments. Why? Well, that's how many tries it took Edison before he successfully found the right filament (wire) to make a lightbulb glow. What if he had quit after nine tries? After ninety? After nine hundred? How about nine thousand? But he didn't give up. Edison wanted to be successful, and he was willing to put the time and effort into getting there. Actually, he probably *enjoyed* the process of trying out his ideas.

Now, we want you to think about the stuff *you* do. Make a list: school projects, music lessons, sports practices.

Now, examine your attitude! Ask a few questions:

- Do you start on a project believing that you can succeed?
- Do you see mistakes as lessons learned or time wasted?
- Is your motto "If at first you don't succeed, try, try again?"
- Are you willing to try? Are you willing to fail?
- Are you willing to try again?

Now, decide you're going to do something better. Put Thomas Edison's picture up where you'll see it a lot, like on the refrigerator or your mirror. When you want to give up, stare at his face. Let him inspire you.

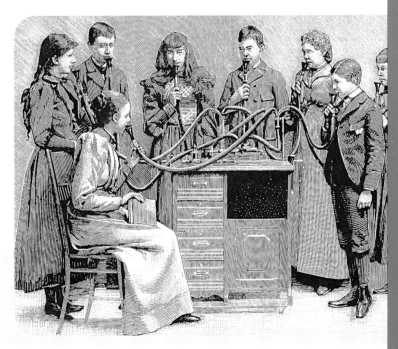

An 1893 etching of Chicago schoolchildren using the recording function of an Edison phonograph—hardly the simple button-pushing process we have today.

ALBERT EINSTEIN

March 14, 1879–April 18, 1955

SCIENCE SUPERSTAR

- **Genius**
- **Physicist (Scientist)**

E=mc². It's probably the most well-known equation in all of science. "Energy equals mass times the speed of light times the speed of light." It may sound like a nonsense phrase to you, but E=mc² unlocked the secret of the atom and led the world into the nuclear age.

It is one of the great contradictions of modern times. Albert Einstein, a man known as a firm supporter of world peace, convinced President Franklin D. Roosevelt to launch a program to build an atomic bomb. The year was 1939, a fateful year for world peace. Hitler's Nazi troops were on the move. Einstein had fled Germany, the country of his birth, years earlier because of its horrible policies against Jews. He had come to America to live in peace.

Einstein knew scientists in his old country had the intelligence to develop atomic weapons, and he knew that Hitler would force them to do so. Should America also build such a weapon of mass destruction? Other scientists and U.S. leaders persuaded Einstein to urge President Roosevelt to act. And so, after many sleepless nights, Einstein wrote a letter. The United States had to build a bomb. Roosevelt agreed. Several days later, Einstein wrote a second letter to the president. He said that when the bomb was developed, it should never be used against people. A demonstration of its awesome power would convince any enemy to surrender.

Dr. Albert Einstein is shown writing out an equation for the density of the Milky Way for the benefit of scientists at the Carnegie Institute, Mount Wilson Observatory.

So August 6, 1945, was a sad day for Albert Einstein. The first atomic bomb was dropped on the city of Hiroshima, Japan. The man of peace saw what he had feared so much come true.

EXPLORE!

You live in a world that can still blow itself up many times over with nuclear weapons. Yes, the terrible Cold War between the United States and the "old" Communist Rus-

Although Einstein was an intellectual whose brilliant and original concepts ushered in the atomic age and changed our vision of the universe, he had many interests beyond physics and mathematics. He was an active pacifist, who warned against the arms race, as well as an accomplished violinist and enthusiastic sailor.

sia is over. Both sides have destroyed some of their bombs, but far too many still exist.

Read Einstein's Power Words carefully. Do you see his meaning? These bombs can still destroy all of us if humans could ever be foolish enough to use them. Einstein knew that if such a thing happened, human society would be taken back to the Stone Age!

You should get busy and learn more about world peace. Why? Because as a future voter, you have to understand what is needed to keep our country and our world safe. Do you think our leaders should work to destroy all nuclear weapons? Or do we need to keep some "just in case" a crazy terrorist gains control of a nuclear bomb?

We hear you. "Hey, I'm just a kid! I'm worried about homework, my clothes, my future." Well, if we don't work to preserve world peace, you may not have a future. Get the picture?

DIVE IN!

Ordinary Genius: The Story of Albert Einstein by Stephanie Sammartino McPherson (Carolrhoda Books, 1997), 96 pages.

POWER WORDS

"I don't know how the Third World War will be fought, but I do know how the Fourth will: with sticks and stones."
—Albert Einstein

BENJAMIN FRANKLIN

January 17, 1706–April 17, 1790

"A MAN FOR ALL AGES"

- **Statesman**
- **Inventor**
- **Author**
- **Diplomat**
- **Scientist**
- **Musician**
- **Philosopher**
- **Public Servant**

"Fish and visitors stink after three days."

Benjamin Franklin was a mastermind at creating one-liners. Franklin enjoyed having fun, and humor was a very important part of his life. His mind was always all over the place, dreaming up new ideas, new inventions, as well as new things to say.

He published many of his words of wisdom in *Poor Richard's Almanac,* which became one of the most popular books in the American colonies. Here's a sampling of "Dr." Franklin's wise and witty sayings:

- "Be slow in choosing a Friend and slower in changing."
- " 'Tis easier to prevent bad Habits than to break them."
- "Glass, China and Reputation are easily crack'd and never well mended."

The book made "Dr." Franklin a wealthy man. And it gave him the money and the time to devote to his many other interests.

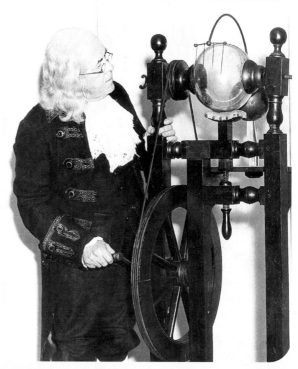

Franklin had a particular interest in electricity, a science that was in its infancy in 1749 when he successfully constructed the world's first electrical battery. He is credited with inventing the word *battery* as well. Here, a model dressed as Franklin demonstrates one of Franklin's early electric efforts.

You probably know about some of the other things he did. Several of them were American "firsts." He founded the first public library, the first postal system, the first volunteer fire company, the first hospital, the first college in Philadelphia (the University of Pennsylvania) and turned the citizens' "Night Watch" into the first Philadelphia police department. Add to that list of accomplishments the "discovery" of electricity in lightning (you know, the kite thing), the invention of the Franklin stove, bifocals, and the lightning rod and many other practical devices.

But we have saved the best for last. Benjamin Franklin is the only person to have signed four of the most important docu-

"Where liberty dwells, there is my country."
—Benjamin Franklin

ments in our country's history. He helped write all four, too. Without these four documents, we might not be the country we are today. Can you name all four? We'll reveal the answers later.

If you're wondering why the title "Dr." appears in quotation marks before Frankin's name, you should know that he awarded *himself* that honor although he never studied for a Ph.D. at a university. That's OK—he earned his degree in the school of life!

EXPLORE!

Though Benjamin Franklin was born in Boston, his adopted city was Philadelphia, Pennsylvania. That's where you'll find The Franklin Institute, an exciting scientific discovery museum. Franklin would have a great time visiting it today. Contact the Institute at:

**The Franklin Institute
Science Museum**
222 North 20th Street
Philadelphia, PA 19103
Phone: (215) 448-1200.
E-mail: webteam@www.fi.edu

A favorite display at the Franklin Institute is a giant human heart. It's so big you can walk through it, following the path that a blood cell traces through the chambers of your heart. In the rotunda of the institute is the Benjamin Franklin National Memorial, where you'll find a 20-foot-high marble statue of the man himself. The Franklin Institute's Web site and literature will tell you more about this fascinating place.

Also look into **Franklin Court** in Philadelphia, where Franklin's house once stood. The house was knocked down in 1812, but today you'll find a "Ghost Structure" there, an oversize steel skeleton that marks that spot. Also at the site are the United States Postal Service Museum, The Franklin Print Shop, and the underground Franklin Museum filled with his inventions.

Now, what about those four important documents that Franklin signed? Well you're probably familiar with the most important ones: the Declaration of Independence and the U.S. Constitution. In between signing them, he helped negotiate and sign the Treaty of Alliance with France, which brought the French army and navy to our side in the Revolutionary War, and the Treaty of Paris, which formally ended that war and recognized the United States as an independent country.

Thanks, Dr. Franklin!

Franklin's most famous experiment involved flying a kite during a thunderstorm in order to prove that lightning is electricity.

JOHN GLENN

July 18, 1921–

THE WORLD'S OLDEST SPACE VOYAGER

- **Astronaut**
- **U.S. Senator**

1962 HEADLINE:
GLENN ORBITS EARTH!

1998 HEADLINE:
GLENN ORBITS EARTH—AGAIN!

It is 1962 and President John F. Kennedy is pinning the NASA Medal on a young John Glenn for his history-making *Friendship 7* spaceflight.

Many of you saw Senator John Glenn board the space shuttle *Discovery* on October 29, 1998, as part of a crew of seven astronauts beginning their nine-day mission. As *Discovery* climbed skyward, a National Aeronautics and Space Administration's (NASA) spokesperson said, "Liftoff for six American heroes and one American legend." And she was right. Because seventy-seven-year-old John Glenn, who became the oldest person in the world ever to travel in space, was legendary.

Back in the 1960s, when President John F. Kennedy committed our nation to sending a manned mission to the moon, Americans loved the idea of exploring the "new frontier." We also loved the idea of entering a space race with our then number-one enemy, the Soviet Union (today's Russia).

On February 20, 1962, we took a big step forward. Alan Shepard, one of the original seven astronauts, flew into space in a suborbital flight. That was great, but it was not the same as the Soviets circling the planet. We were still behind.

Then, in a space capsule called *Friendship 7* (in honor of the seven astronauts), John Glenn closed the gap. Millions of Americans were glued to their television sets as Colonel Glenn's ninety-three-foot

Atlas rocket blasted into space. Inside his tiny capsule, Glenn repeated the final numbers of the countdown: "four, three, two, one, zero, ignition." Liftoff. He was on his way into outer space.

For the next five hours, he circled Earth three times. And Americans worried. Remember, we had never witnessed anything like this before. What if something went wrong? The slightest mechanical failure could mean disaster. Everything had to

DIVE IN!

John Glenn by Thomas Streissguth (Lerner Publishing Group, 1999), 128 pages.

How Do You Go to the Bathroom in Space? by William R. Pogue, John Glenn, and Sidney Harris (Tor Books, 1999), 223 pages.

work perfectly. And everything did. Orbit, reentry, splashdown into the ocean, and America's newest hero had returned safely. The race was on, and America was ready.

EXPLORE!

So much has changed in the space program since it began more than thirty-five years ago. As you explore its beginnings and look at it today, we want you to ask yourself a very important question: Should America spend more or less money on space exploration in the next twenty years than it has in the past twenty years?

In our democracy, "we, the people" have a voice in answering that question through our elected representatives. It's an important question for you because yours is the generation that will be paying for future space exploration. But you have to be well informed to make a sound decision. Start by collecting some space memorabilia (stuff with historical meaning) and books so you can learn about our space program, past and present. Contact:

NASA (National Aeronautics and Space Administration)
300 E Street, SW
Washington, DC 20546
(www:http://www.nasa.gov)

National Air and Space Museum
6th Street and Independence Avenue, SW
Washington, DC 20560
(http://www.nasm.edu/NASMhome.html)
E-mail: mtuttle@ceps.nasm.edu

Goddard Space Flight Center
Greenbelt Road
Greenbelt, MD 20771

"What benefits are we gaining from the money spent? They are probably not even known to man today. But exploration and the pursuit of knowledge have always paid dividends in the long run—usually far greater than anything expected at the outset."
—John Glenn (1962)

"Going back to space, I had defied the expectations for my age."
—John Glenn (1998)

(http://www.pao.gsfc.nasa.gov/gsfc.html)
E-mail: gopher@gophergsfc.nasa.gov

You'll be amazed at how much information these agencies can give you.

If you are interested in more exploration, there's even a Young Astronaut program and NASA-sponsored space camps.

EXPLORE SOME MORE!

For an up-close and personal look at some of the astronauts, pop a couple of videos into your VCR: *The Right Stuff* (about the original seven) and *Apollo 13* (about the moon mission that got into trouble). Both are great movies.

MARTHA GRAHAM

May 11, 1894–April 1, 1991

"A REVOLUTIONARY IN DANCE"

- **Dancer**
- **Choreographer**

It began with a show poster. Martha was almost seventeen when she spotted a poster advertising an appearance of Ruth St. Denis in Los Angeles, about one hundred miles from where the Grahams lived. Martha pleaded with her dad to take her to see this mysterious-looking modern dancer, and he did. He never could have imagined how that one evening would change his daughter's life and the world of dance. Completely overwhelmed by the performance, Martha knew what she wanted to do with her life. "From that moment on, my fate was sealed. I couldn't wait to learn to dance as the goddess did."

Martha's artistic passion and creativity would lead her to study, learn, and eventually found her own dance company because, as she explained, "I did not dance the way that other people danced." Martha Graham moved away from traditional ballet techniques toward a style that communicated intense emotions. She choreographed dances full of energy and spirit. She told stories with movement.

And she stood up for what she believed in, both on and off the stage. In 1936, Graham was invited by Nazi Germany to perform at the Olympic Games in Berlin. She told them to forget it, only to find out later that the Nazis had put her name on a list of undesirable people to be "taken care of" when the Nazis controlled the United States.

Martha Graham danced until she was almost eighty years old. Former First Lady

Martha Graham is known for choreographing sharp, angular movements for her dancers, rather than using the light, graceful positions of classical ballet.

Betty Ford studied with Graham, and so did—Madonna! In 1976, President Gerald Ford called Martha Graham "a national treasure."

EXPLORE!

How open are you to exploring new fields? How daring are you to try things you've never tried before?

DIVE IN!

Martha Graham, A Dancer's Life by Russell Freedman (Clarion Books, 1998), 175 pages.

Martha Graham dances in her *Letter to the World* (1940), based upon the life and poetry of Emily Dickinson. *Letter to the World* reflected the tension between poet and community, a theme that appeared in many of Graham's productions.

When she started to study dance, Martha Graham was twenty-two—older than the other students, a bit overweight, and short. But none of these obstacles to becoming a professional dancer stood in her way.

Have you ever thought about a career in the arts? Use the library and the Internet to learn about dancers, musicians, and singers. See what you have to do to make it in their world.

Each year, in our nation's capital, The John F. Kennedy Center for the Performing

Martha Graham continued to dance into her seventies. She is shown here at age fifty-six, still carrying out her mission, which she was known to describe as "charting the graph of the heart" through movement.

Arts selects five or six living performers to honor for their lifetime achievements. Martha Graham was a Kennedy Center honoree in 1979. It's a great honor, and knowing about what those people have done may inspire you. Some of their names will surely be familiar—Aretha Franklin, Bill Cosby, Bob Dylan, maybe Charleton Heston. Many others are people whose talent and creative energy have set new standards for excellence in the arts. Go to: www.kennedy-center.org for the complete picture on honorees and the Kennedy Center itself, or write to them at

**The John F. Kennedy Center
for the Performing Arts**
Washington, DC 20566-0003
Phone: (800) 472-3556

While you're at it, track down a Martha Graham video or two at the library or video store. Watch her move and know that you are watching history.

51

MATTHEW HENSON

August 8, 1866–March 9, 1955

THE MAN "ON TOP OF THE WORLD"

- **Explorer**
- **Adventurer**

Henson looks a bit haggard in this photo, which was taken after his 1,000-mile trek across polar sea ice, returning from the North Pole. The Inuit who met Henson along his journey called him *Miy Paluk*—kind Matthew.

By 1900 humans had been almost everywhere on this planet's land surface—everywhere, that is, except the North and South Poles.

Adventure: It was in his blood. Risk taking: It was part of his way of life. To escape from a difficult childhood, Matthew Henson set out to sea when only twelve years old. Through "on-the-job" training he learned math, reading, and navigation skills. By the age of twenty-one, he was an experienced world traveler. Then fate stepped in. Henson was working in a fur and supplies store when an explorer named Robert Peary came in to buy some items. He mentioned that he needed a servant to accompany him on an expedition to Nicaragua. Guess whom he chose?

On that trip young Henson so impressed Commander Peary that he made him his trusted assistant. Together, they would try to make Peary's dream come true—to be the first humans to reach the North Pole.

If you like adventure and mystery, there are few stories to match this genuine drama. Constant danger, subfreezing temperatures, wild animals—it was all there. Only after three failed attempts did Robert Peary, four native Inuit (Eskimo) guides, and Matthew Henson finally reach the North Pole. It was April 6, 1909, the end of a torturous thirty-six-day journey. They probably wouldn't have made it at all without Henson. He knew how to drive the dog team and hunt polar bear and musk oxen for food. He realized that the Inuits knew what they were doing in that harsh environment. He learned to speak their language, so he could ask for their help.

The years of hard work and risk taking had paid off. One of the last unreachable points on the globe had been reached. After Henson and Peary's remarkable trek, no one went back to the Pole until seventeen years later, when an airplane flew over it. And no one has ever repeated the trip to and from the North Pole by dogsled.

DIVE IN!

Matthew Henson: Explorer by Michael Gilman (Chelsea House, 1988), 110 pages.

EXPLORE!

For many years, Matthew Henson's achievement was ignored in hisory books because of his race.

Although some people appreciated the key role he played in the North Pole expedition, Robert Peary got most of the glory. People in the early 1900s just weren't ready to cheer for a black man, no matter how big a hero he was.

Some say that Peary turned his back on Henson after they returned from the Pole. When Peary died, he was buried in Arlington National Cemetery and a big monument was placed on his grave. Henson's final resting place was a shared grave in the Bronx, New York.

But America has finally begun to appreciate Matthew Henson. In 1988 he received

"History will take care of that. God will see to it, and God has plenty of helpers."
— Matthew Henson (reflecting on the fact that he had received so little recognition for his role in the successful trek to the North Pole)

a hero's burial in Arlington, right next to his old friend, Peary. In 1997 a book called *Dark Companion* was finally brought back into print fifty years after it was written. It's the only biography of Henson written with Henson himself. See if you can find a copy at your local library. Bradley Robinson was the author, and his son, Verne, has now created a Matthew Henson Web site that is packed with stories, pictures, and tributes to the legendary explorer. Click on: www.matthewhenson.com and take a look. Don't miss the controversy over whether Henson and Peary actually *were* the first to reach the Pole! There's a movie about Peary you can watch, too. It's called *Glory and Honor,* and it came out in 1998. Be sure to watch for it on television or video.

An etching showing that the ice cap over which the expedition traveled was not a smooth snow-covered surface but rather a rugged landscape, fraught with danger.

MILTON HERSHEY

September 13, 1857–October 13, 1945

THE CHOCOLATE KING

- **Entrepreneur (business risk taker)**
- **Philanthropist**

Chocolatetown, U.S.A.: where Chocolate Avenue and Cocoa Avenue meet; where the street lamps are shaped like candy "Kisses"; where the smell of chocolate is everywhere. Sounds like a fantasy place in a kids' book, doesn't it? Well, don't tell that to the people in Hershey, Pennsylvania. It's their home!

Hershey chocolates are world famous—now. But in the beginning, the famous and wealthy Mr. Milton Hershey was a terrible failure in the candy business. First, he failed in Philadelphia. Next, he failed in Denver. Then he failed in Chicago, New Orleans, and New York City. Yes, Milton Hershey racked up failures in some of the greatest cities in the United States. So he returned to Lancaster, Pennsylvania, where he had spent part of his youth. A dear friend lent him some money, and Hershey—believe it or not—*again* tried the candy business. This time he made caramels. Even his mother and his aunt helped him out.

Milton was selling his candy from a pushcart along the streets of Lancaster when a visiting Englishman tasted his caramels. That Englishman happened to be a candy importer, and he *loved* Milton's caramels. He wanted to send lots of them back to England. Suddenly, the Hershey caramel business was booming! Milton made a million dollars. Then he decided to launch a brand-new candy business (choco-

DIVE IN!

Chocolate by Hershey: A Story About Milton S. Hershey by Betty Burford (Carolrhoda Books, 1994), 64 pages. *Creative Minds*

Although he had no children of his own, Milton Hershey generously contributed toward the well-being and education of thousands of children. To this day, the Milton Hershey School offers children free education, housing, clothing, meals, medical/dental care, and recreational activities.

lates) in a brand-new town (Hershey!). And as they say, the rest is history.

EXPLORE!

Hershey, Pennsylvania, is not only home to the leading manufacturer of chocolate products in North America, to an amusement park and Chocolate World attraction, and to other delights, it's also home for Mr. Hershey's kids!

Milton and his wife, Kitty, were unable to have children of their own, so they decided to start a home for orphan boys. Today, the vast complex of homes and schools serves the educational and family needs of over 1,200 children. It's a wonderful continuing memorial to the Hersheys and their desire to use their money to help others. The Hersheys were *philanthropists*. Maybe you've come across this word before. Philanthropists are people who use their money to help others less fortunate than they. The big philanthropists get lots of major credit, like the Hersheys, the Carnegies (built lots of libraries), the Fords, the Rockefellers. Check out philanthropy on the Internet and see what you find.

But you too can be a philanthropist. Buy one less candy bar a week and put that money in a special "Philanthropy Jar." By December holiday time, you'll have enough money in your jar to buy a toy or something else for a child in need. The

POWER WORDS

"I often hear people say that 'children are not what they used to be.' But I have the conviction that they are just what they always have been. Perhaps it is the parents who have changed."
—Milton Hershey

money in your Philanthropy Jar will help you touch someone's life. It's a great start. Your place of worship or community charity groups can help you find a child who needs a present. Write a note to go along with your gift. Encourage that child, whom you've probably never met, to never give up, to keep trying, and to have hope.

That's what Milton and Kitty did. Over the years, their generous philanthropy has given hope to thousands and thousands of boys and girls.

LANGSTON HUGHES

February 1, 1902–May 22, 1967

THE HARLEM RENAISSANCE MAN

- **Poet**
- **Author**
- **Playwright**

Langston Hughes was one of the few writers of the Harlem Renaissance who continued to be an artistic and commercial success after the nurturing environment of the movement ended.

Troubadour is a word that usually refers to a poet-musician from medieval days. But Americans had a troubadour during the Great Depression of the 1930s. He didn't sing, but did he ever read poetry—his own poetry.

You never know when someone else's words may change your life. That's what happened to young Langston Hughes. While he and a friend were on their way to Cuba for a vacation, they decided to stop in Daytona, Florida, to meet the famous African-American educator Mary McLeod Bethune (you'll find her story on page 20 of this book). During their visit, she suggested that Hughes travel throughout the South reading his poetry to earn a living. The idea seemed kind of crazy to him. After all, this was the time of the Great Depression when *everybody* was having trouble finding work. Could he do this? "People need poetry," replied Mrs. Bethune, "especially our people."

Weeks later, while driving back to New York, Langston Hughes made his decision. He would make poetry his career. A friend from his college days would serve as his driver and manager. They would travel through the South, holding poetry readings at colleges attended by African Americans. Langston Hughes wrote and read poetry that spoke of the experience of being black, poetry that taught of the struggles of being black in a segregated America, poetry that

DIVE IN!

Langston Hughes: Poet of the Harlem Renaissance by Christine M. Hill (Enslow, 1997), 128 pages.

Langston Hughes by Milton Meltzer (The Millbrook Press, 1997), 240 pages.

It was while he was working as a busboy in a Washington, D.C., hotel that young Hughes showed his poetry to poet Vachel Lindsay, who in turn announced to local newspapers the discovery of a major new talent.

EXPLORE!

How about writing some poetry?

Me? Poetry? No way! I wouldn't know what to write about.

Take a look at Langston Hughes's poetry. He wrote about who he was, his life experiences. He wrote of being a Negro (the term then used for African Americans), of his travels, his emptiness. Learn from him and write about what you know. Write a poem about your life, a good friend, or a family member who is always there for you. Write about things that scare you, or make you mad, or give you hope. Sometimes Hughes wrote about problems. Give it a try; it's one way of helping yourself see a problem clearly and maybe finding a way to solve it.

Whether to share your poetry with others is a decision only you can make. Langston Hughes decided to share his, but some poets keep their work completely private or share it only with a close friend. Whatever you do with it, write it. Follow Langston Hughes's lead and allow your inner voice to speak.

gave a voice to a better life for black Americans. And everywhere he spoke, the audiences, mostly African-American college students, greeted him eagerly. He reached them. His words stirred them, angered them, made them proud.

Langston Hughes joined other writers who led an African-American cultural movement centered in New York. That movement was called the Harlem Renaissance, and Hughes became one of its most well-known troubadours. Like the troubadours of medieval days, he moved among his people, spreading a message.

POWER WORDS

"Hold fast to dreams, for if dreams die, life is a broken-winged bird that cannot fly."
—Langston Hughes

THOMAS JEFFERSON

April 13, 1743–July 4, 1826

AUTHOR OF THE DECLARATION OF INDEPENDENCE

- **U.S. President**
- **Statesman**
- **Author**
- **Architect**
- **Inventor**

On what day of the year did Thomas Jefferson die? Look at the top of the page. See it? Does that date ring a bell? A "Liberty Bell" maybe? Thomas Jefferson died on the Fourth of July, known as Independence Day since 1776, when he wrote and our founding fathers signed the Declaration of Independence. Kind of ironic, isn't it? Jefferson's last day on the planet was the fiftieth birthday of the nation he helped create. And get this: Thomas Jefferson's good friend John Adams, the other man most responsible for that Declaration, died the very same day!

Thomas Jefferson was almost seventeen when he entered the College of William and Mary in colonial Virginia's capital, Williamsburg. Jefferson had always liked school. It wasn't unusual for him to spend fifteen hours a day studying, although he was definitely not an eighteenth-century book-

In writing the Declaration of Independence, Jefferson carefully balanced the strength of government against the freedom and well-being of the individual.

worm. He loved horse racing, card playing, dancing, and playing the violin.

Teachers are powerful people. Good teachers can change your life, and that's what happened to young Thomas Jefferson in college. Dr. William Small was a professor of mathematics and science. He gave Jefferson a love for learning how things work. For the rest of his life, Thomas Jefferson would try to understand *everything*: plants, animals, mechanical things, buildings. Dr. Small's influence eventually led his student to design a beautiful home called Monticello. Another teacher, lawyer George Wythe, became his law professor. Jefferson called him "my second father." Mr. Wythe taught the future author of our Declaration

DIVE IN!

Thomas Jefferson: The Revolutionary Aristocrat by Milton Meltzer (Franklin Watts, 1991), 256 pages.
Thomas Jefferson by Wendle C. Old (Enslow, 1997), 128 pages.

" . . . All men are created equal, that they are endowed by their Creator with certain unalienable Rights, that among these are Life, Liberty and the pursuit of Happiness."

—Thomas Jefferson (from the Declaration of Independence)

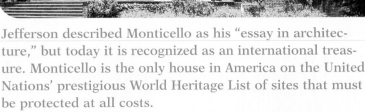

Jefferson described Monticello as his "essay in architecture," but today it is recognized as an international treasure. Monticello is the only house in America on the United Nations' prestigious World Heritage List of sites that must be protected at all costs.

of Independence the principles of law found in that great document. And in 1776 teacher George Wythe became one of the fifty-six brave signers of his former student's greatest work, the Declaration of Independence.

EXPLORE!

Write your own epitaph. An epitaph is a statement about you that is carved on your tombstone. Tombstone? Why should you be thinking about a tombstone? You're young and have your whole life ahead of you. But what you do with that life will affect how people remember you when you're gone.

Thomas Jefferson wrote his own epitaph. Of all his many accomplishments, he wanted us to remember three specific things he did during his incredible life:

- authoring the Declaration of Independence
- authoring the Virginia Statute for Religious Freedom
- founding the University of Virginia

You can see his grave and tombstone when you visit **Monticello**, the magnificent home he designed. To find out more about Monticello, contact the Visitors' Center at

PO Box 316
Charlottesville, VA 22902
Phone: (804) 984-9822 or
On the Web: www.monticello.org

We know you've probably thought about what you want to do when you are an adult—most kids wonder about their futures. Maybe you've pictured what career you'll have or how much money you'll make. But look at Jefferson's epitaph again—he didn't even list any of his jobs (like president, vice president, secretary of state). He listed what he considered to be the greatest gifts he gave to the American people. What important things do *you* want to accomplish in life? Raise a family? Write poetry? Volunteer for a charity? Learn to paint? Life's rewards can be measured in so many meaningful ways. Maybe making money *is* important to you. How will you do it? With honesty or deceit? With compassion or ruthlessness? You decide.

Thinking about what you *really* want people to see on that tombstone later can help you make some important life choices now.

HELEN KELLER AND ANNE SULLIVAN

Keller: June 27, 1880–June 1, 1968   Sullivan: April 14, 1866–October 20, 1936

"THE MIRACLE WORKERS"

- **Author**
- **Teacher**
- **Activists**

Helen Keller's writing career spanned fifty years. In addition to *The Story of My Life*, she wrote eleven other books and numerous articles on blindness, deafness, social issues, and women's rights.

Water. It's necessary for all life. You drink it, bathe in it, swim in it. It's always there. For Helen Keller and her teacher, Anne Sullivan, it was the word and the substance that changed their lives.

Born in Alabama more than a hundred years ago, Helen began life like any other child. But before her second birthday, a terrible illness robbed her of sight and hearing. Suddenly, this bright, curious little girl was trapped in a world without light or sound. Although Helen tried to communicate using signs she invented herself, she knew that other people did many, many things that she could not. And it made her angry.

As Helen grew older, she grew angrier. She would explode into kicking, screaming temper tantrums every day. Her parents desperately wanted to help her, but they didn't know how. Then Anne Sullivan came into their lives. A teacher from a school for the blind, she moved in with Helen's family, determined to bring Helen's world back to life again. Anne was strict, but caring. She encouraged Helen to

POWER WORDS

"I knew then that 'w-a-t-e-r' meant the wonderful cool something that was flowing over my hand, That living word awakened my soul, gave it light, hope, joy, set it free!"
—Helen Keller

use her remaining senses to experience the world around her. She taught her to spell words with her fingers ("water" was the first), recognize objects by touch, and read Braille. Helen even learned to speak.

Now, Helen wanted to try *everything*. She rode horses, swam, took walks in the woods, and learned to row a boat. She graduated with honors from Radcliffe, a prestigious college for women. She wrote and lectured about being deaf and blind. Helen had found her way out of the dark.

For forty years Helen Keller and Anne Sullivan trav-

Helen Keller (left) and Anne Sullivan are pictured around 1894, when Helen was still a teen. Later, Helen was to become the first deaf-blind person to graduate from college. Throughout those years, Anne Sullivan laboriously spelled books and lectures into her pupil's hand.

Helen Keller National Center (HKNC) for Deaf-Blind Youth and Adults

111 Middle Neck Road
Sands Point, NY 11050.

They'll send you lots of information about helping deaf-blind people manage in a seeing and hearing world. Read their literature, then check out your own environment. Does your town have beeping traffic lights? (What are *they?*) Are elevators equipped with Braille numbers? Does your school teach anything about sign language or Seeing Eye dogs? Is there anything you can do to make your community more accessible to *all* its citizens? Write or E-mail us if you come up with a project and make it happen.

Also, rent the movie *The Miracle Worker* or borrow it from your library. In this 1962 film, two Oscar-winning actresses portray Helen Keller and Anne Sullivan. You'll cringe when Helen explodes into fits of rage. You'll cheer when she realizes that objects have names that you can spell with your fingers. You'll learn the significance of "w-a-t-e-r" to young Helen. Don't miss this classic!

eled around the world, helping the public overcome its fear of physically challenged people. Presidents invited Keller to the White House. Foreign governments showered her with honors. When Anne Sullivan died in 1936, Helen Keller mourned the passing of her friend, but continued to travel and inspire.

Helen Keller was eighty-seven years old when she died in 1968. She never saw the audiences who marveled at her abilities and her spirit. She never heard their applause. She only felt their love and respect.

EXPLORE!

How easily could vision- or hearing-impaired persons find their way around your school or neighborhood? Do you even know what their needs are? Contact the

DIVE IN!

The Story of My Life by Helen Keller (Bantam Doubleday Dell, 1991), 225 pages.

Helen Keller by Dennis Wepman (Chelsea House, 1991), 112 pages.
American Women of Achievement

JACKIE JOYNER-KERSEE

March 3, 1962–

OLYMPIC CHAMPION

- **Athlete**
- **Humanitarian**

She was born when the civil-rights campaign for black Americans was in full stride. She grew up in an America wrestling with change, where thousands of ordinary citizens, black and white, were fighting racial discrimination and insisting that all people should have equal rights to life, liberty, and the pursuit of happiness.

Home was a crime-infested neighborhood. "I was constantly surrounded by chances to do wrong," she said. Success seemed a distant dream. But young Jackie Joyner was something special. When she came into the world, her grandmother insisted that she be named Jacqueline, after Jacqueline Kennedy, who was the U.S. First Lady at the time. Why? "Because," she said, "someday this girl will be the first lady of something."

At the age of nine, Jackie competed in her first track meet and finished last. But she didn't give up. She practiced and ran, setting goals, determined to be the best she could be. She didn't even let asthma slow her down. (Asthma is an illness that makes it very hard for you to breathe.) In 1986, Jackie married her coach, Bob Kersee. When she was twenty-six, Jackie Joyner-Kersee won two gold medals at the Olympics; four years later, she added another. Her specialty? The grueling heptathlon in which each contestant takes part in seven challenging track and field events. Many call her the world's greatest living female athlete.

EXPLORE!

One year before her victory at the 1988 Olympic Games, this dynamite athlete established the **Jackie Joyner-Kersee Foundation** to help city youth develop their talents and reach their potential. To find out more, write to: 500 East Broadway, PO Box 6349, East St. Louis, IL 62201. Phone: (618) 482-2200. You can also check the Internet for current information on the project. Use your favorite search engine to track it down. What does the JJK Foundation do? For starters, it gives money for college scholarships and provides mentors for inner-city youth. Its major goal, however, is to rebuild the Mary E. Brown Community Center in East St. Louis, where Jackie grew up. That center was a second home for young Jackie.

Jackie wants the new center to be bigger and better, with a library, arts-and-crafts rooms, and, of course, athletic facilities. And it will, she hopes, bring

POWER WORDS

"I remember where I came from, and I keep that in mind. . . . If the young female sees the environment I grew up in and sees my dreams and goals come true, they will realize their dreams and goals might come true."

—Jackie Joyner-Kersee

Jackie Joyner-Kersee's expression shows the pride and joy she was feeling as she accepted the heptathlon gold medal in the 1992 Olympics. The grueling event involves a 200-meter run, 100-meter hurdles, high jump, and shot put one day; long jump, javelin, and 800-meter run the next.

young people and senior citizens together to make her hometown a better place to live! So check out the Web site and maybe you'll get ideas on how to become involved in your local area. Remember, our country works because individual citizens make it happen. Jackie Joyner-Kersee believes in "bringing something back to the community." Why not follow the lead of a champion? What can you do to bring something back to your school, neighborhood, or community?

Jackie said it best: "Don't follow in my footsteps. MAKE YOUR OWN!"

EXPLORE SOME MORE!

Approximately 15 million Americans suffer from asthma, so chances are you know someone who has it. Jackie Joyner-Kersee has it. Maybe you have it yourself. Find out more about it by visiting the American Medical Association Asthma Information Center at www.ama-assn.org/special/asthma/support/resource/resource.htm. Or contact the

American Academy of Allergy, Asthma and Immunology
611 East Wells Street
Milwaukee, WI 53202
www.aaaai.org
E-mail: edi@execpc.com

The information they send might help you or a friend find new ways to clear the hurdles asthma puts in front of you.

DIVE IN!

Jackie Joyner-Kersee by Geri Harrington (Chelsea House, 1995), 120 pages. *Great Achievers—Lives of the Physically Challenged*

Jackie Joyner Kersee: Superwoman by Margaret Goldstein (Lerner Publishing Group, 1994), 56 pages. *Achievers*

THE REVEREND DR. MARTIN LUTHER KING JR.

January 15, 1929–April 4, 1968

"THE VOICE OF EQUALITY"

- **Civil Rights Leader**
- **Minister**
- **Humanitarian**
- **Recipient, Nobel Peace Prize**

The Reverend Dr. Martin Luther King Jr. delivered his famous "I Have a Dream" speech on the steps of the Lincoln Memorial in Washington, D.C., on August 28, 1963.

Would you let angry people throw tin cans and rocks and rotten eggs at you? Would you let a powerful fire hose spray water on you and knock you down, bruising and hurting you? Would you let dogs bite you? Would you tolerate any of these things and not fight back?

The children of Birmingham, Alabama, endured all these things because they believed in the powerful words of the Reverend Dr. Martin Luther King Jr. Still powerful today, in the 1960s they were the words that made most Americans realize that racism had to end. You probably think we mean most *adult* Americans. No, we mean kids, too.

Dr. King was arrested on Good Friday, 1963. He spent one of the Christian world's major holy days, Easter Sunday, alone in a jail cell. There, he wrote a famous letter, explaining why the civil-rights protestors must fight hate with love. The city was filled with racial hate, and children wanted to be part of the protests. Should he allow them, knowing that some of them could get hurt?

DIVE IN!

I Have a Dream: The Life and Words of Martin Luther King, Jr. by Jim Haskins (Millbrook Press, 1992), 112 pages.

For three nights after his release from jail he lay awake, trying to decide. Eventually, he knew the answer. "The children and grandchildren are doing it for themselves." They should take part.

And so, when Birmingham's marches for equality and justice resumed, there they were. First, teenage girls, then elementary school children, then high-school boys joining in the protests. Horrible things happened to them. Hundreds were arrested. And all of it was seen on television. A horrified America saw the ugly face of racism

"Free at last! Free at last! Thank God Almighty, we're free at last!"
— The Reverend Dr. Martin Luther King Jr.

against children. And Americans finally realized that the time had come to listen to the words of Martin Luther King Jr.

EXPLORE!

Few people in our country's brief history (remember, we are a young nation by history's standards) have been as powerful with words as was Dr. King. His speeches helped to bring alive our Declaration of Independence's key phrase: ". . . all men are created equal."

Read a portion of his famous "I Have a Dream" speech, proclaimed on August 28, 1963, at the Lincoln Memorial—or, better yet, *listen* to it. Obtain a video from your library or video store about the civil-rights movement of the 1960s. His thrilling speech will be on it. It also appears with Dr. King's biography in the CD-ROM version of many encyclopedias.

You'll understand why, as a nation, we have honored Dr. King with a national holiday—January 15, his birthday. You'll understand why, in 1964, he was awarded the Nobel Peace Prize. Dr. King's widow, Coretta Scott King, has continued to carry on the struggle for civil rights through the **Martin Luther King, Jr. Center for Nonviolent Social Change.** The King Center is located at

449 Auburn Avenue, N.E.
Atlanta, GA 30312
Phone: (404) 524-1956

Also access the center's Web site at www.thekingcenter.com to find lots of information about Dr. King as well as links to many related sites. Contact the King Center and request a complete copy of "I Have a Dream." Pick out a favorite paragraph and memorize it. As you speak the words, think carefully about the meaning for you and how in your life you can work to deal with all people equally.

(For more inspiring words, see Explore! for Mary McLeod Bethune on page 21.)

On December 10, 1964, Martin Luther King Jr. received the Nobel Peace Prize, in Oslo, Norway. Almost thirty years later, his acceptance speech still rings with hope. ". . . I accept this award on behalf of a civil rights movement which is moving with determination and a majestic scorn for risk and danger to establish a reign of freedom and a rule of justice. . . ."

ROBERT E. LEE

January 19, 1807–October 12, 1870

THE GENERAL FROM VIRGINIA

- **General**
- **College President**

Try to imagine the tough decisions the founders of our country had to make. The men and women in colonial America were loyal subjects of the king of England. But they decided to make their lives better by ending that relationship. The people we call American patriots—George Washington, Thomas Jefferson, Benjamin Franklin—were actually traitors to the throne.

Eighty years later, Colonel Robert E. Lee of Virginia had to make a similar difficult decision. In the spring of 1861, our country was falling apart as Southern states seceded (withdrew) from the Union. Virginia was one of those states. The new president, Abraham Lincoln, pledged to keep the country united, even using military force if necessary. To lead the troops, he turned to Colonel Lee, considered by many of his peers to be the "greatest soldier alive."

Uncertainty tormented Lee. What should he do? Be a loyal American and lead the Union army, or be loyal to family, friends, and Virginia and take up arms in support of his state? Lee decided to stand with his beloved Virginia. Eventually, he would command Confederate troops in the Civil War. His men would fight bravely, but the Union would prevail. After four years of conflict, Lee would surrender. So why should you learn more about Robert E. Lee? Because he had courage and integrity.

Lee was a complex man with strong beliefs, who *had* to be true to those beliefs. Choosing Virginia over the Union was not

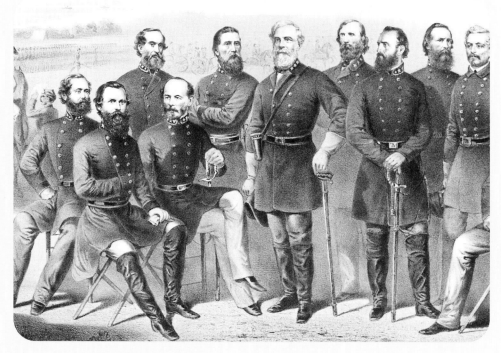

General Robert E. Lee, shown here surrounded by his generals, has been called the greatest military genius America has ever produced. To this day, his campaigns are almost universally studied in military schools as models of strategy and tactics.

"It is well that war is so terrible. We should grow too fond of it."
—Robert E. Lee (after the Battle of Fredericksburg in December 1862)

DIVE IN!

Robert E. Lee: Southern Hero of the Civil War by Mona Kerby (Enslow, 1997), 129 pages. *Historical American Biographies*

Virginia's General: Robert E. Lee and the Civil War by Albert Marrin (Atheneum, 1994), 192 pages. Illustrated.

EXPLORE!

Americans young and old are fascinated by the Civil War. Although it took place more than 130 years ago, many people talk about it, read about it, visit its battlefields and museums, and even reenact it. Check with your local historical society to see if there is a Civil War reenactment group in your area. You may want to attend one of their events or even join.

To get you started in learning about the many interesting people involved in that great struggle, watch Ken Burns's first-rate, award-winning video series called *The Civil War*. All ten episodes are tremendous. Then, start reading. Choose biographies, historical fiction, novels, picture books, and magazines. Yes, there are even monthly magazines devoted to coverage of the Civil War.

Here are a few books to look for that will plunge you into the midst of the war between the states:

The Tamarack Tree by Patricia Clapp (Lothrop, Lee & Shepard, 1986)

The Borning Room by Paul Fleischman (HarperCollins, 1991)

Across Five Aprils by Irene Hunt (Follett, 1964)

Voices from the Civil War by Milton Meltzer (HarperCollins, 1989)

The Boys' War by Jim Murphy (Clarion, 1990)

Shades of Grey by Carolyn Reeder (Macmillan, 1989)

Red Cap by G. Clifton Wisler (Lodestar, 1991)

the only painful decision he had to make. Later on, when the Confederate army was suffering major defeat, Lee was under a lot of pressure to keep on fighting, to go underground if he had to. But Lee was convinced that to continue the war was pointless. As hard as it was, he had to stand by what he believed was best for his troops and the Confederacy. Surrender was hard to swallow, but sending more men to die in battle was unthinkable.

Lee is shown astride Traveller, his horse that he rode throughout the Civil War.

MERIWETHER LEWIS, WILLIAM CLARK, AND SACAGAWEA

Lewis: August 18, 1774–October 11, 1809   Clark: August 1, 1770–September 1, 1838
Sacagawea: c. (circa)1786–c. 1812 or 1884*

"TRAILBLAZERS"

• Explorers

It was one of the greatest bargains of all time. For a mere $15 million, President Thomas Jefferson bought the entire Louisiana Territory from the French Empire under Napoleon. At three cents an acre, America was the proud owner of 828,000 acres.

To find out about our new addition, President Jefferson sent army captains Meriwether Lewis and William Clark, along with thirty-one soldiers, on an expedition to explore the land from the Northern Great Plains (around St. Louis, Missouri) to the Pacific Ocean. This "Corps of Discovery" faced two years and four months of blizzards and bears, floods and hunger, illness and uncertainty. Survival depended upon their ingenuity and ability to live off the land.

For all their skill and courage, Lewis and Clark would probably have had an even harder time without a young Indian woman named Sacagawea (sometimes spelled Sacajawea). She was a teenager and pregnant when the explorers hired her French-born husband to help guide their expedition west. Throughout the journey, she served as interpreter, negotiated for horses when the explorers needed them, added to the travelers' diet with roots and plants, and showed incredible strength and courage. She and her newborn son, traveling with thirty-three men, also served as a symbol of peace to the native tribes they encountered along the way.

This venture into the West opened new chapters in our nation's history. The team of Lewis, Clark, and Sacagawea had indeed blazed a new trail.

* There's some disagreement about how long Sacagawea lived. Some historians think that she died when she was twenty-five. However, according to Shoshoni oral history, Sacagawea lived a much longer life, calling herself Porivo. Porivo was active with the Shoshoni and died at the age of ninety-six. Which version do you think is true? Can we ever know for sure?

Sacagawea, with her infant Jean Baptiste, was the only woman to accompany the thirty-three members of the permanent Lewis and Clark expedition to the Pacific Ocean and back.

"... *as no woman ever accompanies a war party of Indians in this quarter. A woman with a party of men is a token of peace.*"
—William Clark
(from his journal)

EXPLORE!

True or false: The expedition of Lewis and Clark and Sacagawea was of immense benefit to the peoples of North America. You're right! It's a trick question.

Our country was still very young, and white settlers were eager to move and acquire new land. But the land they wanted was already inhabited by Native Americans. So, the Lewis and Clark expedition clearly brought different results for different people. The positive consequences for one group were negative consequences for another.

To encourage you to think about these heroes and this historical dilemma, we want you to start a journal. That's what Lewis and Clark did during their travels. Find a book or Web site that includes the explorers' journal entries. You'll need some accurate background to get a feel for the time period and setting. In your journal, climb into the skins of different people involved in the expedition.

One of the ways we can bring great historical people to life is by "walking a mile in their moccasins." Your journal will help you do that. We would like to read some of your journal, if you don't mind sharing. It would be interesting to see how different kids in different parts of the country view the journeys of Lewis, Clark, and Sacagawea.

Books that may help get you started on your journal include:

All About Me: A Keepsake Journal for Kids by Linda Kranz (Rising Moon, 1996). This book gets you going by asking you questions about yourself.

Emma's Journal—The Story of a Colonial Girl by Marissa Moss (Silver Whistle, 1999), Young America Voices Series. This is an example of a journal written by someone from another time period.

A Book of Your Own: Keeping a Diary or Journal by Carla Stevens (Clarion, 1993). This book offers examples of diary entries.

Don't forget! A new Sacagawea dollar is in circulation! Contact the **U.S. Mint** at 633 3rd Street NW, Room 715, Washington, DC 20220 or on the Web: www.usmint.gov to learn all about how this explorer was chosen to appear on our latest dollar coin.

Another woman in this book of heroes has already appeared on a dollar coin. Do you know who?

DIVE IN!

Across America: The Story of Lewis and Clark by Fiona MacDonald and David Salariya (Franklin Watts, 1998), 32 pages.

Sacagawea: Westward with Lewis and Clark by Alana S. White (Enslow, 1997), 128 pages. *Native American Biographies*

ABRAHAM LINCOLN

February 12, 1809–April 15, 1865

"THE GREAT EMANCIPATOR"

- **U.S. President**
- **Orator**
- **Legend**

Compassionate, brilliant, courageous, determined, strong, *honest*—heroic words come easily to mind when we think about Abraham Lincoln. His face and profile are probably the most recognized of any American hero. Close your eyes and you can picture him immediately. "Honest Abe" is as much a part of all of us as is our flag, the Fourth of July, the Statue of Liberty, and our fifty states. He's the man who freed the slaves and saved the Union.

Since you've probably already learned more at school about Abraham Lincoln than most of the other heroes, we'll try to tell you something about him you might not already know. He was the first U.S. president to grow a beard. And it's all because of a letter from an eleven-year-old girl.

Grace Bedell lived in Westfield, New York. Shortly before the election of 1860, when the country was having real trouble because of the slavery issue, she wrote to candidate Lincoln with some advice. She told him that growing a beard would help him win because " . . . you would look a great deal better for your face is so thin. All the ladies like whiskers and they would tease their husbands to vote for you." *

Lincoln shown with his beloved son Tad, who died at the age of eighteen. Lincoln's life was filled with personal tragedy in that only one of his four sons lived to maturity.

Well, Lincoln took young Grace's advice. It's doubtful his decision to grow a beard made a difference in the voting. Remember, there were no TV news bulletins to announce "Lincoln Grows Beard!" But her influence did certainly change how everyone from 1860 to the present day remembers and pictures Abraham Lincoln. Isn't it amazing the difference a simple letter can make?

---

* Women were not allowed to vote in 1860. Another of our 50 American Heroes helped change that. Do you know who she is? Hint: A question in the Lewis, Clark, and Sacagawea section of this book has the same answer.

DIVE IN!

Where Lincoln Walked by Raymond Bial (Walker & Co., 1998), 48 pages.

Lincoln: A Photobiography by Russell Freedman (Clarion, 1987), 160 pages. Illustrated.

" . . . and that government of the people, by the people, for the people shall not perish from the earth."
—Abraham Lincoln

We hope you know that the Power Words are found at the end of the Gettysburg Address, one of the most famous speeches ever given. President Lincoln wrote the speech and delivered it on November 19, 1863, in Gettysburg, Pennsylvania. The entire speech lasted only two minutes! Do you know how the speech begins?

incidents from his life that show his compassion, courage, and all the rest. As you read these stories, you'll discover something about the man. You'll discover that President Lincoln the legend was a real human being. Each story you find will help you appreciate how genuinely good he was. You'll see him as a legend. You'll see him as a human being. You'll see him as an example of how you can live your life.

EXPLORE!

Legend!

If you look at all our 50 heroes and the words we use to describe them, the only time we used the word "legend" was with Abe. He was very special, but we also want you to know that he was just like you and us. And to help you prove that to yourself, we have a task in mind. Take the six adjectives we listed for Lincoln (compassionate, brilliant, courageous, determined, strong, and *honest*) and find a story about him that illustrates each word. Dig into the books written about him and the tons of Lincoln-related sites on the Internet. Uncover

EXPLORE SOME MORE!

The most famous monument ever built to honor Abe Lincoln is probably the Lincoln Memorial. You can see it if you visit Washington, D.C., but if you can't, you'll find it at: www.nps.gov/linc It's an awesome tribute to an awesome man. The monument is made of marble, granite, and stone.

The Lincoln Memorial includes a statue of Lincoln that is 19 feet high, as well as carved inscriptions from his Gettysburg Address and his Second Inaugural Address.

YO-YO MA

October 7, 1955—

THE WORLD'S FINEST CELLIST

- **Musician**
- **Educator**
- **Musical Ambassador**

DIVE IN!

My Son, Yo-Yo: A Biography of the Early Years of Yo-Yo Ma by Marina Ma and John A. Rollo (University of Michigan Press, 1995)

Music. It's almost everywhere. You dance to it, march to it, worship through it, celebrate with it . . . and many of you make it—you are musicians. Meet one of the world's greatest musicians—Yo-Yo Ma.

Can you remember what you were doing when you were five years old? Yo-Yo Ma was giving his first public cello recital. That's right, at the age you were finger painting in kindergarten, he was playing an instrument in front of an audience. A cello, by the way, is a stringed instrument, larger than a violin but smaller than a string bass.

Yo-Yo Ma has become a world-famous ambassador for classical music. He travels everywhere and plays with great orchestras and other famous musicians. He has made more than forty-five albums. Thirteen of them have been honored with Grammy awards.

He is always trying to find new and different ways to reach more people with classical music. In the early 1990s, Yo-Yo Ma teamed up with Bobby McFerrin for a pretty unusual performance in Boston. McFerrin is a jazz musician who uses his voice as an instrument. The pair teamed up with the Boston Philharmonic and put together a concert of all kinds of music—classical, fun, mournful, and lighthearted.

And Yo-Yo Ma does not think classical music is just for grown-ups either. He has taken his cello to *Sesame Street* and *Mister Rogers' Neighborhood*. Maybe you saw him when you were little. Whenever he goes on a concert tour, he schedules time to teach students, both musicians and nonmusicians. He also encourages young people to create music, and he teaches them how. He has also been known to share his instruments with them. The cellos that Ma plays are very valuable, worth hundreds of thousands, even *millions* of dollars. But on more than one occasion, he has invited young cello students to experience the thrill of playing one of his practically priceless instruments. This is what Yo-Yo Ma does. He loves music so much that he wants to share it with the world.

EXPLORE!

Music can build bridges of understanding between cultures. In many ways, it is the truest international language. We can enjoy a song even if we don't understand the words. Yo-Yo Ma's talents are so special because each time he draws his bow across the strings

"I just want to take music to wherever it can go, to people who are open."

—Yo-Yo Ma

of his cello, he reaches across cultures, across generations, across types of music. He makes music universal. Play a Yo-Yo Ma CD or tape. As you listen to his extraordinary performance, think of the many types of music you probably have never listened to. Then look for some. We want you to explore music from other cultures. You may be able to do it on your computer (if it comes with the right bells and whistles). Or you can borrow CDs and tapes from your local library or your school's music teacher. Or ask your friends who have a different cultural background to share their music.

Then listen. Really listen. Why? Because appreciating the music of others helps you to appreciate them as well. Understanding and tolerance begin by learning to see that "different is okay." Different music—from whatever culture—is okay, just different. Different people—from whatever culture—are OK, just different. Simple.

So begin letting Yo-Yo Ma's beautiful music lead you to be more accepting of everybody's music. And of everybody.

Yo-Yo Ma is one of those rare superstars who continues to care so much about the future of music that he will teach children in the schools. Here he is giving an onstage workshop for the children of the Peabody School in Cambridge, Massachusetts.

73

GEORGE C. MARSHALL

December 31, 1880–October 16, 1959

ARCHITECT OF PEACE

- **Army Chief of Staff**
- **Secretary of State**
- **Recipient, Nobel Peace Prize**

President Harry S Truman called General George C. Marshall "the greatest of the great of our time." High praise, but do you even know who George C. Marshall was?

In 1953, for the first time ever, the Nobel Peace Prize was given to a professional soldier. Why? Because General George C. Marshall came up with a plan that saved war-torn Europe from starvation and despair after World War II. Whole cities and towns had been destroyed. Bridges, roads, homes, and schools were gone. Two years after the war, Europe was still having trouble getting back on its feet. The Marshall Plan would offer U.S. aid for recovery, but not only to our World War II allies. We would help our former enemies, too, if they let us.

Don't miss this point: For the first time ever in the history of the world, the victors offered to help the vanquished! In a speech at Harvard University on June 6, 1947, Marshall said: "[Without] the return of normal economic health in the world . . . there can be no political stability and no assured peace." He continued: "Our policy is directed not against any country or doctrine, but against hunger, poverty, desperation, and chaos." Marshall knew that if things went on as they were, hungry Europeans would look for help elsewhere, even if their helper gave food with one hand and took freedom and justice away with the

President Harry S Truman (*right*) awards an Oak Leaf Cluster to the Distinguished Service Cross to General Marshall upon his retirement as chief of staff.

other. If they had to turn to Eastern Europe's Communist dictators for aid, that's exactly what would have happened.

Well, the Marshall Plan worked. Our enemies refused help (they didn't want to play by our rules), but the rest of Europe recovered and peace prevailed. Years later, when he accepted his Nobel Prize, the frail, seventy-three-year-old general spoke of democracy's greatness, but warned that these democratic principles "do not flourish on empty stomachs."

"There must be an effort of the spirit—to be magnanimous, to act in friendship, to strive to help rather than to hinder."
— General George C. Marshall (in a lecture given on the day after he accepted the Nobel Peace Prize in 1953)

EXPLORE!

One of the world's greatest honors is to be awarded the Nobel Prize for Peace. To date, sixteen Americans have been so honored; five of them are found in this book: Marshall, Jane Addams, The Reverend Dr. Martin Luther King Jr., Theodore Roosevelt, and Elie Wiesel. Use the Internet or library reference section to find the names of the other winners.

Did you know that Nobel Prize winners receive a cash award? Jane Addams gave hers to the Women's International League for Peace and Freedom. Dr. King donated his $54,600 prize to the civil-rights movement. Roosevelt distributed his prize to various charities, and Elie Wiesel founded The Elie Wiesel Foundation for Humanity with the $290,000 he received from the Nobel Committee. No one is quite sure what George Marshall did with his prize money

DIVE IN!

George C. Marshall: A General for Peace by Alan Saunders and John A. Scott (Facts On File, 1995), Photographs. *Makers of America*

of $33,840, not even the researchers at the **George C. Marshall Foundation,** an organization dedicated to "preserving and promoting . . . the ideals and values of disciplined selfless service, hard work, integrity and compassion of George Catlin Marshall." Check out the George C. Marshall Foundation at: www.gcmarshallfdn.org or contact them at PO Box 1600, VMI Parade, Lexington, VA 24450. Phone: (540) 463-7103.

What would *you* do with the money if you won the Peace Prize? Would you use it to promote peace? How? Write or E-mail us with your ideas.

This mural depicting the spectrum of Marshall's achievements hangs in the auditorium of the George C. Marshall Museum in Lexington, Virginia.

JOHN MUIR

April 21, 1838—December 24, 1914

FATHER OF OUR NATIONAL PARKS

- **Conservationist**
- **Author**
- **Naturalist**

Even as a boy, John Muir loved nature. Plants and animals fascinated him. His first glimpse of lightning bugs after the family came to America from Scotland was thrilling. However, John was also a practical, hardworking person. After attending college for a while, he was not sure what he wanted to do with his life. He was a "tinkerer"—an inventor. Maybe he would create new machines.

One day, while he was working in a factory, a sharp piece of a metal file flew into his right eye. Suddenly, he was blinded. Within a few hours, his entire world was dark. For a month Muir faced a future of total uncertainty. Then, amazingly, his sight returned. What he regained was more than his eye vision. John Muir found his life's vision. "God has to nearly kill us sometimes to teach us lessons," he said. The wilderness—that was where Muir really wanted to be. Not in a factory in some city. But in nature, exploring and learning everything he could.

All of us have benefited from John Muir's transformation. As he traveled, he became the champion of preserving the magnificent places we now value as our national parks.

DIVE IN!

John Muir: Saving the Wilderness by Corinne J. Naden (The Millbrook Press, 1992), 48 pages. *Gateway Biography*

In 1901, Muir wrote *Our National Parks*, the book that brought him to the attention of President Theodore Roosevelt. In 1903, Roosevelt (*left*) visited Muir in Yosemite. It was there that they collaborated on what were to become Roosevelt's innovative conservation programs.

EXPLORE!

John Muir's favorite place was Yosemite, a beautiful California landscape of mountains and waterfalls. Saving it to be one of our great national parks is part of his legacy. But he also *lost* a conservation battle—a battle to save the equally beautiful Hetch Hetchy Valley, part of the Yosemite region. That river was dammed to provide San Francisco with water. Now, nearly one hundred years later, John Muir's struggle is being refought. And you can join in.

"Whenever we try to pick out anything by itself, we find it hitched to everything else in the universe."
—John Muir

As a wilderness explorer, John Muir was known for his solo excursions in California's Sierra Nevada mountains, among Alaska's glaciers, and to Australia, South America, Africa, Europe, China, Japan, or anywhere in the world that would afford him the opportunity to bask in the unspoiled beauty of nature.

First, learn about the situation by contacting the Sierra Club, founded in 1892 by John Muir and his friends. Ask the club members for information about the current effort to return the Hetch Hetchy Valley to its natural condition. Do you agree with their opinion? What do their opponents argue? Become an informed player in this conservation conflict.

Why bother? Because someday, you may be lucky enough to visit Yosemite and maybe see Hetch Hetchy, too. And even if you don't, you'll know that your voice joined others in letting decision makers know what America wants. That's what our country is all about—every citizen, young or old, being heard.

By the way, the Sierra Club can give you lots of neat information on John Muir and other national parks. Contact the **Sierra Club** at 85 Second Street, Second Floor, San Francisco, CA 94105-3441. Phone:

(415) 977-5500. On the Web: www.sierraclub.org Also, contact the **U.S. National Park Service** at 1849 C Street NW, Washington, DC 20240. Phone: (202) 208-6843. You can learn all about protecting our great wilderness heritage.

Although his work took place more than a century ago, John Muir remains our nation's most famous and influential naturalist and conservationist.

SANDRA DAY O'CONNOR

March 26, 1930–

FIRST WOMAN U.S. SUPREME COURT JUSTICE

- **Supreme Court Justice**
- **Wife**
- **Mother**

What's it like to be "the first" to do something? Maybe you were the first in your family to learn to tap-dance. Maybe you were the first among your friends to learn to rollerblade. If so, then you're like Sandra Day O'Connor, the first woman ever appointed to the U.S. Supreme Court, the most important group of judges in the country.

Being the first isn't always the easiest way to go. If you're the first, you must be able to handle all the responsibilities and all of the problems that go with it. Sometimes people are slow to accept "the first," because they're just not used to it. When she first became a lawyer, law firms in San Francisco and Los Angeles rejected Sandra Day O'Connor. She was a woman, and the legal world wasn't used to women in the courtroom. It didn't matter how good or smart she was. But O'Connor persisted, and her persistence paid off. Becoming the first woman on the highest court in the land rep-

Justice O'Connor shattered the idea that women were not qualified to serve on the Supreme Court—and as a role model, further opened the door for women at all levels of the legal profession.

resented acceptance and a step for all women on the road to equal rights.

Oh, there's one more important "first" in Justice O'Connor's lifetime of firsts. Her family. She did the juggling of career, home, and kids that many moms today have to do. She was a full-time mother for a while when her three boys were very young. Then, when she resumed the practice of law, she established priorities, and commitment to

DIVE IN!

Meet My Grandmother: She's a Supreme Court Justice by Lisa McElroy, with help from Courtney O'Connor and Joel Benjamin (The Millbrook Press, 1999), 32 pages.

Sandra Day O'Connor by William Peter Huber (Chelsea House, 1992), 111 pages. *American Women of Achievement*

"Whether your future work is in business, in government, or as a volunteer, try to set your sights on doing something worthwhile and then work hard at it."
—Justice Sandra Day O'Connor

family remained at the top of the list. Though history will surely focus on her accomplishments in Washington, D.C., we shouldn't only admire her for her Supreme Court job. She is so much more than that. Justice O'Connor is a wife, a mother, a grandmother, a citizen, a *person*—and a terrific role model for young women.

A hero.

EXPLORE!

To many Americans, the U.S. Supreme Court is a mysterious place. The magnificent building across the street from the U.S. Capitol is open to the public, but few people visit it. Why? Maybe because we think of courtrooms as boring. There certainly aren't any airplanes hanging from the ceiling as in Washington's Air and Space Museum. Or maybe we think that what goes on in the Supreme Court's courtroom doesn't really affect our lives. Wrong!

The Supreme Court makes our Constitution a "living document." Sandra Day O'Connor and her eight fellow justices interpret that 1787 document and apply it to our lives. Today. The Supreme Court's Public Information Office has some cool information to share, including an illustrated booklet about the Court, who's on it, and what it does. There are also copies of actual Supreme Court decisions, visitors' guides to the Supreme Court and to an Oral Argument of the Court, as well as a list of books and resources that might interest kids your age. Contact:

Supreme Court of the United States Public Information Office
1 First Street NE
Washington, DC 20543
Phone: (202) 479-3000

You can also check out the *Young Oxford Companion to the Supreme Court of the United States*, a book by John J. Patrick (Oxford University Press, 1994) or, click onto http://www.oyez.nwu.edu/tour for a tour of the Court.

To keep track of what's on the docket at the Supreme Court (what they're discussing), keep an eye on the TV news or newspaper. Something the justices rule on today could affect you in a big way tomorrow. The law is *real*, and the way judges interpret it can change your life. Pay attention!

Her own children now grown, Justice O'Connor is a devoted grandmother. If you would like to learn more about the justice from her granddaughter Courtney, see the *Dive In!* section.

ROSA PARKS

February 4, 1913–

"MOTHER OF THE CIVIL RIGHTS MOVEMENT"

- **Civil Rights Activist**

Did you ever drop a pebble into a pool of water? The pebble makes waves, watery circles hundreds of times larger than the pebble itself. You might call Rosa Parks a kind of "pebble dropper." She was an African-American woman who, on December 1, 1955, refused to give up her seat on a city bus to a white man. That simple deed created waves that reached way beyond the Parks's home in Montgomery, Alabama. She had tossed a pebble that would change the pool forever.

Back in the 1950s, many states including Alabama kept "Jim Crow" laws on the books. These laws kept whites and blacks apart in almost all public areas, including city buses. White people were allowed to sit in the front, and black people had to go to the back of the bus, to the "colored" section. If more whites boarded the bus, then blacks had to stand and give their seats in the back to the whites. Simple rules. Everyone followed them. It was the law. But Rosa Parks broke the law.

On that day, this hardworking seamstress said *no* when the bus driver ordered her to give up her seat. She had worked all day and she was tired. Too tired to walk home as she usually did to avoid the indignity of the segregated bus. More important,

POWER WORDS

"Some people think I kept my seat because I'd had a hard day, but that is not true. I was just tired of giving in."
—Rosa Parks

though, was the other kind of tired she felt. She was tired of giving in. So, she didn't. Rosa believed that the question of where to sit on the bus was not a little thing. The angry bus driver didn't think it was a little thing either. He called the police, and Rosa Parks was arrested.

Was she scared? Of course she was. She knew how blacks were treated in the city jails. But she knew it was time to take a stand for what she believed was right.

Rosa Parks understood the meaning of the words in both the Declaration of Independence and the Constitution. It was time to make the words about equality work for *every* American. This courageous woman's simple deed led to a major boycott of city buses in Montgomery. It would soon become the rallying point for the civil-rights movement that was just beginning to attract attention.

Rosa Parks's simple act of courage was going to change America.

EXPLORE!

A single, simple act of courage. For Rosa Parks, it was simply refusing to give up her seat; for teenager Ryan White, it was simply refusing to hide from those who viciously discriminated against him because he had AIDS. Instead, he chose to teach the world about the disease that would claim his life. For black Olympic athlete Jesse Owens, it was simply going to Berlin in 1936 and running gold-medal-winning races as Adolf

Rosa Parks, now in her eighties, is still active in fighting racial injustices and sharing her message with others.

Hitler and the white supremacist Nazis watched in disbelief. These people faced unfair treatment and ugly hatred with the dignity and courage of heroes.

Do you know any stories like this? Tell us about someone who stood tall when things were rough. Zero in specifically on people who have battled discrimination and hatred, like Rosa Parks, or AIDS victim Ryan White, or Olympic athlete Jesse Owens. The people you tell us about may be famous, but they don't have to be. Scan your own family, community, or school for single acts of courage. Tell us about the dance teacher who stopped kids from name-calling the boys who wanted to dance. Or the aunt and uncle who talked you and your friends out of bad-mouthing kids from another neighborhood.

Write or E-mail us with your stories. Keep them simple, but be clear about that act of courage. Let us know how we can contact you, too. If we receive enough inspiring stories, we'll publish another book, with *you* as the authors. A book about courage. A book about heroes you know whose courage has made this world a better place.

DIVE IN!

Rosa Parks: My Story by Rosa Parks with Jim Haskins (Dial, 1992), 192 pages.

A Supreme Court decision struck down the Montgomery, Alabama, ordinance under which Rosa Parks had been fined, and forever outlawed the long-ingrained practice of racial segregation on public transportation.

I. M. PEI

April 26, 1917–

MASTER BUILDER

- **Architect**
- **Dreamer**

Ieoh Ming (I. M.) Pei's father wanted him to become a doctor, but the sight of blood made him sick. He liked buildings; maybe he could try architecture. He decided to study in the United States; he thought American movies were cool. Who knew that this teenager from Shanghai, China, would become I. M. Pei, the master builder?

His buildings have astonished millions of people around the world:

- The beautiful East Building of Washington, D.C.'s, National Gallery of Art;

- The "glass pyramid" at the Louvre Museum in Paris (that's where the Mona Lisa is kept);
- The seventy-four-story Bank of China skyscraper in Hong Kong;
- Even the Rock and Roll Hall of Fame Museum in Cleveland, Ohio!

Almost half of I. M. Pei's building designs have won major awards. In 1993, President George Bush awarded him the Presidential Medal of Freedom. Throughout his brilliant career, Pei lived up to his name, Ieoh Ming, which means "to inscribe brightly." What a smashing success story! All gain and no pain!

Well, almost. There *was* pain—*panes* actually. Like all people who achieve great things, I. M. Pei had his share of failures. The panes that caused him pain were in the

Although Pei's redesign of the entrance to the Louvre was initially controversial, the 66-foot-tall glass and iron pyramid in the entryway has become synonymous with the Paris museum.

DIVE IN!

I. M. Pei by Aileen Reid (Knickerbocker, 1998), 112 pages.

John Hancock Tower in downtown Boston, Massachusetts. Built in the early 1970s, this tallest of Boston's skyscrapers was covered by pale blue sheets of glass. "Magnificent!" said the critics. The citizens of the city hailed this breathtaking structure . . . until the panes of glass started falling out!

But every problem has a solution *if* you don't give up. The panes were replaced with a more reliable type, and the pain of failure gave way to a renewed spirit of confidence. I. M. Pei had proven again what so many other heroes learned in their careers: Never, ever give up. No pain, no gain!

EXPLORE!

Among the trophy case full of honors that Pei has won is the Pritzker Architectural Prize. Some people call it the "Nobel Prize of architecture." Pei used the $100,000 prize money to set up a scholarship fund for Chinese students wanting to study architecture in the United States. The students then return to China to practice their profession. When they do, they can visit sites like Fragrant Hill, outside of Beijing. There, they'll see a hotel that Pei designed in the 1980s, nearly forty years after he left China. Although he had been in America since he was a teenager, Pei had remained tuned in to the relationship between nature and buildings that is important to the Chinese people. He designed Fragrant Hill with that relationship in mind, and it serves to inspire young architects in his homeland.

"What you have learned and experienced in life comes out in a very unplanned way."
—I. M. Pei

Today, there's a major movement in America to make sure that great buildings are preserved. Children born even a hundred years from now should have an opportunity to see I. M. Pei's architectural wonders. Check out the Internet and search for "Preservation" efforts. Look for great buildings (like the Empire State Building in New York), whole sections of cities (like the colorful Art Deco section of Miami Beach), and off-the-wall roadside stuff (like the very first McDonald's Golden Arches). You might even get involved in saving America's great architecture for your grandchildren!

A stunning piece of daring architecture, the Rock and Roll Hall of Fame and Museum is situated on the shore of Lake Erie in downtown Cleveland, Ohio.

CHRISTOPHER REEVE

September 25, 1952–

"A SUPER MAN"

- **Activist**
- **Actor / Director**

Superman: In the movies, he could fly; in real life, he moves around in a wheelchair. In the movies, he crusaded against crime; in real life, he crusades for a cure for spinal-cord injuries. In the movies, nothing but Kryptonite could hurt him. In real life, pain is very much a part of his life. In the movies, people admire and respect him because he is good. In real life, people admire and respect him because he is good.

Reeve was a celebrity. Handsome, talented, athletic—life had been good to him, and he knew how to make the most of everything life had to offer. As an actor, Christopher Reeve appeared in more than a dozen movies, a dozen more TV movies, and more than one hundred plays. Many people first knew him as "Superman," the fictional Man of Steel whom he played in several films. But acting wasn't Christopher Reeve's only passion. He was also an ardent political and social activist, an accomplished pianist, an airplane pilot, and an outstanding athlete. He loved sailing, scuba diving, skiing . . . and horseback riding. That's what he was doing on Memorial Day in 1995. That's when the thoroughbred he was riding in competition came to a 3-foot-high jump and stopped—just stopped. Reeve tumbled over the horse's neck. His hands were tangled up in the bridle. He couldn't break his fall. His head hit the ground. The impact fractured vertebrae in his spine and instantly paralyzed him from the neck down. He couldn't even breathe on his own. At that moment, life as Christopher Reeve had known it was over.

His body was broken, but the accident couldn't crush the *real* Christopher Reeve—his mind, his spirit, his drive. He was starting out on an inspiring journey, and he was going to take us all with him. On the journey, he would meet strong, inspiring people with problems much like his own. He would call them heroes. "I think a hero," he said, "is an ordinary individual who finds the strength to persevere and endure in spite of overwhelming obstacles."

Millions of people know the story of Christopher Reeve's courage, and millions

Though he is paralyzed from the neck down, Christopher Reeve has turned out to be more of a hero than even Superman, whom he once portrayed in the movies.

84

have learned more about the prevention and cure of spinal-cord injuries because he has been our teacher. With his wife, Dana, by his side, he is raising money for research and working to rebuild his own body, too. Reeve has set a tremendous goal for himself—to stand and walk by his fiftieth birthday in the year 2002. Will it happen? He thinks it will. So does his family. And so do we. We believe in this super man.

EXPLORE!

You can help this courageous "super man." Yes, *you!* First, let him know you're on his side. Write him a letter. Tell him that his efforts have made a difference in the way you look at spinal-cord injuries and physically challenged people. Write to his wife, Dana Reeve, as well. Her husband's accident changed her life forever, too. A lot of people would have gotten scared and backed away, but Dana Reeve had the guts to stay by her husband's side and begin a new life with him. We could all learn something from her. Read *Care Packages: Letters to Christopher Reeve From Strangers and Other Friends* by Dana Reeve (Random House, 1999). You'll see what others have written to this courageous couple.

Now get involved by learning about spinal-cord injuries. Contact the

American Paralysis Association
500 Morris Avenue
Springfield, NJ 07081
Phone (800) 225-0292

Or try contacting

The Christopher Reeve Foundation
PO Box 277
FDR Station
New York, NY 10150-0277
Phone: (888) 711-HOPE

Tap into the Christopher Reeve Homepage on the Internet to find other links, avenues, and ideas on how you can raise money for research or help in other ways.

One of the best ways you can get involved is by learning how to prevent spinal-cord injuries. If you play sports, follow the rules, play a clean game, know what you're doing, and *wear protective gear*. If you ride in or drive a car, *wear a seat belt*.

And while we're on the subject of safety, head injuries can also leave you disabled forever. When you ride your bike or rollerblade, *do you wear a helmet*? Do you know how many kids are permanently injured every year because they thought helmets were dorky or uncomfortable or they "just forgot?" Well, how comfortable do you think it is to sit in a wheelchair attached to a respirator?

POWER WORDS

"We should never walk by somebody who's in a wheelchair and be afraid of them or think of them as a stranger. It could be us—in fact, it is us."
—Christopher Reeve

CAL RIPKEN JR.

August 24, 1960–

IRON MAN

- **Athlete**
- **Humanitarian**

Big deal. He never missed a day of work. Well, when you really think about it, it is a big deal. In fact it's one of the most incredible records existing in any sport—more important than the number of home runs hit in a season and more special than a tally of touchdowns, goals, or baskets scored. The record we're talking about belongs to "Iron Man" Cal Ripken Jr. He played 2,632 baseball games in a row with the Baltimore Orioles. He did not miss a single game in sixteen years! That's like having perfect attendance in elementary school, junior high, senior high, and college!

Cal actually broke the record for consecutive games on September 6, 1995. The old record was 2,130—set way back in 1939 (See Explore Some More to find out who set it). But on that special night, the record was going down. In front of 46,272 screaming fans, Cal took to the field to play game number 2,131. We wonder how many times during all those years Cal played even when he didn't feel like it. Maybe his shoulder ached, or he had a cold, or he was just having a bad day. But no matter what, he put on a great show for his fans. Wonder when he realized that his love for baseball would lead him into the record books?

Some people have said, "So what—all he did was show up for work." Maybe so. But if what he did was that easy, guys would be breaking that record all the time. And, besides, Cal didn't just show up for work—he showed respect for himself, his teammates,

Shortstop is a key position, and Cal took great pride in his fielding. He never took a play for granted.

his fans, and the game of baseball by giving 100 percent every time out, for sixteen solid years. We think that's something to celebrate. By the way, on that special night, number 2,131, Cal also hit a home run.

EXPLORE!

If you like sports statistics, we're sure you'll want to look at all the records that Cal holds. You can bet he'll be in the Baseball Hall of Fame as soon as he is eligible. But his records alone don't make him one of our 50 heroes every kid should meet. It's his *character*, and that's what we want you to explore.

"In my elementary school 'autobiography' I wrote, 'Reading is essential to become a baseball player. You have to be able to read a contract and other important papers.' True enough, but you have to be able to read proficiently, period. . . ."

—Cal Ripken Jr.

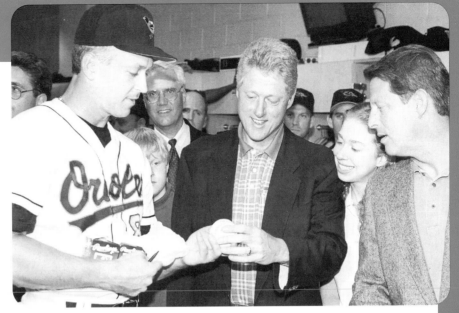

Cal attracted a lot of attention and admiration for his achievement of becoming baseball's new "Iron Man." The fans gave him a 22-minute ovation, and President Bill Clinton attended the record-setting game.

What is "character"? It's not something you can touch or hold. It's who you are—your values, how you treat others, the good things you do. And here's where Cal is a real recordholder, too.

Lots of athletes charge kids for their autographs. Cal's autographs are free. Lots of athletes like to grab your attention by acting like maniacs. Cal is a gentleman on the field and a devoted family man off the field. Lots of athletes play their sports mainly for the money they can make. Well, Cal probably likes to make a buck, too, but he also plays because he truly loves the game. And he donates money and time to help others.

We want you to learn about the **Ripken Learning Center** in Baltimore, Maryland,

which Cal and his wife set up in 1990 by donating $250,000. Its mission is to help adults learn to read. Check out its Web site. It's just one example of the *character* that sets the Iron Man apart from all the rest.

EXPLORE SOME MORE!

As Cal approached the magic number of 2,131, he knew he would be breaking the record held by one of baseball's most beloved and courageous players. This incredible man made a nation weep when illness forced him to leave the game he loved. Rent the classic baseball movie "The Pride of the Yankees" and learn the story of the larger-than-life player who considered himself "the luckiest man on the face of the earth"—Lou Gehrig.

DIVE IN!

Cal Ripken Jr.: My Story by Dan Gutman, Mike Bryan, and Cal Ripken Jr. (Dial Books for Young Readers, 1999), 128 pages.

JACKIE ROBINSON AND BRANCH RICKEY

Robinson: January 31, 1919–October 24, 1972

Rickey: December 20, 1881–December 9, 1965

"TEAM PLAYERS"

- **Baseball Champions**
- **Civil Rights Trailblazers**

You probably can't conceive of an all-white major league baseball team. But in 1946—not that long ago—all of the sixteen major-league teams were "for whites only."

Today it is hard to believe that our country had to be dragged kicking and screaming into the world of equality on the playing field. And two guys who loved baseball helped drag us there.

Go back to 1947. Baseball was *the* national pastime. At the time, there were two different baseball leagues. No, not the National League and American League. We're talking about the major leagues and the Negro leagues. Only white ballplayers could play in the majors, and dream of making it to the World Series. Black players, no matter how good they were, played in their own league and were "kept in their place" as second-class athletes.

Then Branch Rickey came along. He was the president and general manager of the Brooklyn (now the Los Angeles) Dodgers,

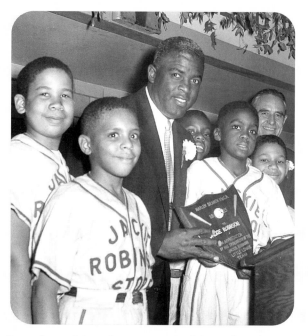

Once he achieved success, Jackie Robinson didn't forget the battles that remained to be fought by young black kids. Here he is awarded a plaque by the Jackie Robinson All Stars.

and he thought things had to be changed. He knew there were black men who played ball as well as white men, and he knew they should be playing in the big leagues. But he also knew that segregation was a part of baseball and a part of America. To integrate the game would not be easy.

Rickey determined that Jackie Roosevelt Robinson was the man who could survive the ordeal that integrating baseball would be. In late August 1945, shortly after the end of World War II, Rickey met with Robinson and asked him to join the Dodgers' farm team (the Montreal Royals) to prepare for the major leagues. Robinson was going to make history. This extraordinary

DIVE IN!

First in the Field: Baseball Hero Jackie Robinson by Derek T. Dingle (Hyperion Books, 1998), 48 pages

Jackie Robinson by Richard Scott and Nathan I. Higgins (editor) (Chelsea House, 1987), 124 pages

meeting was one of the most dramatic episodes in sports. Many people believed in segregation and hated black Americans. Rickey warned Robinson that if he decided to go through with this, he would be deliberately attacked. If he lost control, the people who opposed integration would pounce on his display of anger, no matter how justified, and push the whole effort back to square one. At one point during their meeting, Robinson could no longer contain himself. He said, "Mr. Rickey, are you looking for a Negro who's afraid to fight back?" With passion in his voice, Rickey replied, "I'm looking for a ballplayer, Jackie, with guts enough not to fight back."

Robinson joined the Royals, then the Dodgers, and Rickey was right. Fans, players, coaches, even some of his own teammates reacted with hate. But Robinson held on and played the game—the baseball game. And he played it very, very well.

The integration of our national pastime was a major step toward the integration of our society.

Both Robinson and Rickey went on to earn places in the Baseball Hall of Fame. And places in history as well.

EXPLORE!

Jackie Robinson and Branch Rickey integrated baseball, but how about other sports? Did white and black people always

play on the same football and basketball teams? How about sports like swimming, tennis, and ice skating? Pick a sport (or several) and do a little research. You might be surprised at how recently discrimination existed in some professional sports. For example, in 1997, Tiger Woods won the Masters Tournament, one of the biggest prizes in men's professional golf. Yet, as late as 1974, no African Americans had played in that major golf event. In fact, the "whites only" clause in the Professional Golfers Association (PGA) was not erased until 1961.

Each time a color barrier falls, we witness a sign of progress toward achieving greater equality and mutual acceptance in this country. So, check out some sports encyclopedias and see if you can identify heroic athletes of color who were the first to integrate your favorite sports. Let us in on their stories of courage and determination.

Who knows—maybe you'll uncover a hero for our next list of 50!

POWER WORDS

"A life is not important except in the impact it has on other lives."
—Jackie Robinson

"I couldn't face God much longer knowing that his black creatures are held separate from his white creatures in the game that has given me all I own."
—Branch Rickey (speaking to his grandson)

ROY ROGERS AND DALE EVANS

Rogers: November 5, 1911– July 6, 1998   *Evans: October 31, 1912–February 7, 2001*

KING OF THE COWBOYS
QUEEN OF THE WEST

- **Parents**
- **Humanitarians**
- **Movie Stars**
- **Singers**
- **The most popular cowboy and cowgirl the world has ever known**

"**H**appy trails to you until we meet again."

"Happy trails to you. Keep smiling until then."

Ask your parents or grandparents if they ever sang along with this song. Ask them if they remember the singing "King of the Cowboys," his "Queen of the West," and a horse named Trigger.

A singing cowboy and the queen of the West? In a book about heroes? What were we thinking?

In many ways, Roy Rogers and Dale Evans are our choices for national unsung heroes. What they represent is so precious in life that we hope you'll value what they valued. Commitment stands out first. The couple made a promise to love, honor, and obey one another when they said their marriage vows. For fifty-one years, until Roy's death, they kept those vows. They kept the promises they made to one another. Devotion to their beliefs also identifies Roy Rogers and Dale Evans. They were devoted to their country, to their faith, and to the basic goodness of people. They were proud to let others know of their strong convictions. They stood up for what they believed in. Finally, the two of them showed us how to be unselfish. Of particular concern to them were severely abused and neglected children. **The Happy Trails Children's Foundation** reaches out to rescue more of those kids today. Roy Rogers and Dale Evans helped others.

Although Roy Rogers and Dale Evans were movie superstars, they made tons of public appearances, always taking time to visit sick children and shake the hands of their young fans. Life was not always easy. Both endured the loss of people they loved, including three of their children. But through it all, Roy Rogers and Dale Evans remained strong, optimistic, and generous people. Heroes.

POWER WORDS

"No amount of fame or money can equal the feeling of watching sick children's faces light up when I visited them in the hospital."
—Roy Rogers

EXPLORE!

We have a challenge for you. Roy Rogers and Dale Evans are included in this book because they stood for important values. They were superstars in their day, but when fame faded, their inner goodness still shone brightly. What about the superstars of today?

Roy and Dale are shown here with five of their children. The family eventually grew to include nine children, four of whom were adopted.

for achievements; the celebrity for well-knownness. . . . Time makes heroes but dissolves celebrities." We think twenty-five years from now, Roy Rogers and Dale Evans and their commitment, devotion, and unselfishness will still be known. Tell us which of today's big names will be remembered twenty-five years from now. Not for their freakiness or the number of hotel rooms they trashed. But for the good and decent way they led their lives.

The ones you all know about? Besides their talent for making music, acting, or playing sports, what makes them good people?

Do the superstars you scream for do admirable things like Roy Rogers and Dale Evans did and continue to do through their foundation? Do the superstars you idolize stand for decent values? Do they want to? Basketball player Charles Barkley once said that he didn't want to be anybody's role model. Should we expect him to be? There are probably some terrific people among today's celebrity headliners. Tell us about them.

A famous current historian (his name is Daniel Boorstin) said: "The hero is known

DIVE IN!

Happy Trails, Our Life Story by Roy Rogers and Dale Evans with Jane and Michael Stern (Simon and Schuster, 1995), 252 pages. Photographs.

Known as the King of the Cowboys, Roy Rogers starred in nearly one hundred movies. This is his classic movie publicity shot, waving to his fans as he balances astride his famous horse, Trigger.

ELEANOR ROOSEVELT

October 11, 1884–November 7, 1962

"FIRST LADY OF THE WORLD"

- **Humanitarian**
- **Diplomat**
- **First Lady**

Somehow this formal White House portrait of an elegantly gowned First Lady is totally atypical of the hands-on social activist whom we remember as Eleanor Roosevelt.

Lonely, sad, afraid—these words barely begin to describe Eleanor as a child. But this shy little girl couldn't stay frightened forever. Not when others were feeling excluded and unwanted, too.

America in the 1930s was a racially divided land. Many white citizens blindly carried on their parents' and grandparents' prejudices against people of color. But not Eleanor Roosevelt. She was the wife of a popular president, Franklin Delano Roosevelt (FDR), who led our country through the Great Depression and World War II. Eleanor believed with all her heart the words of our Declaration of Independence: that all people are created equal and have equal rights ("life, liberty, and the pursuit of happiness"). And while being afraid was part of her childhood, Eleanor wasn't afraid as an adult to stand up for her beliefs.

For example, in 1939, African-American singer Marian Anderson was to perform at Constitution Hall in Washington, D.C. She was an incredibly gifted opera singer. But some of the members of the Daughters of the American Revolution (DAR) objected to a black person singing in their auditorium and canceled the performance. Eleanor, a lifelong member of the DAR, was outraged. She immediately quit the group, then helped arrange a new location for the concert. On Easter Sunday, Marian Anderson proudly sang in front of the Lincoln Memorial, and 75,000 people came to listen.

During that same year, Eleanor attended a meeting in Birmingham, Alabama, where state law forbade whites and blacks to sit together in public places. Well, she simply refused to obey the law and sit on the "white side" of the meeting room. Instead, she had a chair placed in the room's center aisle. There she sat, showing the Alabama legislators what she thought of their segregation laws.

Eleanor's life reflected her commitment to public service in our country and throughout the world. As FDR's wife, she energized and transformed the role of First Lady. Later, as his widow, she served as a delegate to the United Nations and kept on with her human-

Although she was controversial in her day, history has appreciated Eleanor Roosevelt's tremendous contribution to her husband's presidential legacy.

POWER WORDS

"No one can make you feel inferior without your consent."
   —Eleanor Roosevelt

itarian work: always fighting racial injustice, working tirelessly for social reform—and earning the title "First Lady of the World."

At the time of her death, the shy, lonely, scared little girl was the most recognized individual in the world.

EXPLORE!

While our Constitution doesn't even mention the role of a president's spouse,* we are always interested in the chief executive's family. The First Lady in particular can draw a lot of attention to a special cause. Eleanor Roosevelt transformed the role of First Lady by using her position to embrace the world. Have others followed in her footsteps? Use your library or the Internet to research first ladies of the last fifty years. What were their interests and concerns?

* Remember, someday a woman may be president. If she's married, will we call her husband the "First Gentleman"?

DIVE IN!

Eleanor Roosevelt: A Life of Discovery by Russell Freedman (Clarion, 1993), 198 pages.

Stateswoman to the World: A Story about Eleanor Roosevelt by Maryann N. Weldt (Lerner, 1992), 56 pages.

How did they draw attention to important issues of the day, like literacy, the war on drugs, historic preservation, and the beautification of America?

What do you think *today's* First Lady should work on? As you read about the 50 amazing people in this book, a particular idea or cause connected with one of these heroes may catch your attention. Should today's First Lady promote Jackie Joyner-Kersee's program for young athletes? Or Christopher Reeve's quest for a cure for spinal-cord injuries? Tell her what you think! Contact her at

The White House
1600 Pennsylvania Avenue
Washington, DC 20500
On the Web: www.whitehouse.gov
E-mail: first.lady@whitehouse.gov

FRANKLIN D. ROOSEVELT

January 30, 1882–April 12, 1945

MR. PRESIDENT

• **U.S. President**

Franklin D. Roosevelt was well known for his frequent "fireside chats," which were informal radio talks. It was his way of explaining his programs directly to the American people, and thus eliciting their support.

The man who would four times be elected president of the United States, who led our nation through the Great Depression and World War II, spent the last twenty-four years of his life in a wheelchair.

Polio was his crippler. Usually this disease affected children, which is why it was also called infantile paralysis. It struck Franklin when he was thirty-nine years old, a father of five children and well into his national political career. This personal tragedy changed FDR's life forever. He had to focus on learning how to live in a wheelchair. The man who had loved to hike, play tennis, and sail now depended on other people to dress and undress him.

It was more than a physical challenge he faced. He had to deal with the mental challenge, too. Franklin had lived a life of luxury and privilege.

As a privileged young man at Groton, a private school, Franklin had been influenced by his caring headmaster (principal) the Reverend Endicott Peabody. Reverend Peabody wanted the wealthy boys to provide leadership and public service for others not as fortunate.

Now privileged Franklin felt helpless. Now he could truly understand what his headmaster had meant. When he became president, the Great Depression had left one-third of all Americans hungry and homeless. He vowed to help these unfortunate people in any way he could. FDR's leadership and his charisma (his personal magnetism) led our country through some of its most troubled times.

EXPLORE!

Here's an opportunity for you to become an oral historian, someone who learns about the past by talking to people who lived it. You find out what they know about people and events of long ago by asking them good

DIVE IN!

Franklin Delano Roosevelt by Russell Freedman (Clarion Books, 1990), 208 pages.

Franklin D. Roosevelt: The Four-Term President by Michael A. Schuman (Enslow, 1996). 128 pages.

" . . . So first of all let me assert my firm belief that the only thing we have to fear is fear itself. . . ."
—Franklin D. Roosevelt

questions. After you read more about FDR, try it.

Most likely, your grandparents or great-grandparents, your older uncles and aunts, elderly neighbors, and friends were alive when FDR was our president. Ask them how they felt about him. Did they listen to his "fireside chats" on their radios? Did they like how he led the country? Did they cry when they heard the news that he had died? Ask if they knew that FDR was in a wheelchair, unable to walk. Are you surprised by that question? Well, most Americans in the 1930s and 1940s did *not* know this about their president. That's because newspaper photographers and filmmakers agreed not to show him in a wheelchair. The press was free to do so, but they didn't. Why do you think they made that decision?

Record your interviews on cassette tapes or video. Of course, you can take notes of your conversation, but you have to be very careful to make sure you write down exactly what the person is telling you.

Mail or E-mail us your oral history of FDR so we can learn from you.

EXPLORE SOME MORE!

Bring this gigantic historical figure alive for yourself in two special ways. First, rent the video *Sunrise at Campobello* and watch it.

Next, visit in person or via the Internet the places important in Franklin's and his wife Eleanor's (also one of our heroes) lives. They include **Franklin's home** and presidential library at Hyde Park, N.Y. Phone: (914) 229-8114; his

Little White House and Museum
in Warm Springs, Georgia
Phone: (404) 655-3511

and his cottage in

Campobello International Park
(Campobello Island)
New Brunswick, Canada
Write to: PO Box 97
Lubec, Maine 04652

or

PO Box 9
Welshpool, New Brunswick
EOG 3HO

If you visit Washington, D.C., be sure to see the newest monument to a president, the FDR Memorial. It was controversial in that the sculptor portrayed the president in his wheelchair, although barely visible from under his cloak.

THEODORE ROOSEVELT

October 27, 1858–January 6, 1919

"THE CONSERVATION PRESIDENT"

- **U.S. President**
- **Conservationist**
- **Adventurer**
- **Nobel Peace Prize Winner**

After his return from the war in Cuba, Colonel Roosevelt posed for this photograph at Montauk, Long Island. When he later described in detail how he looked and dressed in the war, he said, unlike this image, "In Cuba I did not have the side of my hat turned up."

In the late 1800s and the early part of the twentieth century, the Industrial Age changed the United States. More people came to America and built cities and towns. Teddy Roosevelt realized that all this progress could devour the American wilderness if we weren't careful. A good friend of his named John Muir (he's on our list of 50 heroes, too) talked to TR about the need to preserve our national wilderness. Teddy Roosevelt became the first U.S. president to take major action to protect the environment.

During his seven and a half years in the White House, TR designated 150 national forests, 55 bird and game preserves, 5 national parks (including Yosemite) and 18 national monuments, like the Grand Canyon. Though an avid hunter, he once said: "More and more, as it becomes necessary to preserve the game, let us hope that the camera will largely supplant the rifle." More than sixty years later, in honor of Teddy Roosevelt's devotion to preserving natural America, the National Wildlife Federation awarded him first place in its Conservation Hall of Fame.

But Teddy Roosevelt wasn't only a giant in the world of conservation. He was also a dynamo in a hundred other ways. Before he became president, TR was colonel of the Rough Riders during the Spanish-American War, governor of New York, a police commissioner, and a sheriff. Did you know he was also a founder of the Intercollegiate Athletic Association, which is now the National Collegiate Athletic Association (NCAA)? He ran a ranch out West, traveled all over the world, and raised six kids. He also managed to write thirty-five books and more than *150,000* letters to tons of people.

DIVE IN!

Bully for You, Teddy Roosevelt! by Jean Fritz (G. P. Putnam's Sons, 1991), 128 pages. Illustrated.

Theodore Roosevelt and his America by Milton Meltzer (Franklin Watts, 1994), 191 pages.

Like Roosevelt himself, the first family was young, energetic, and a novelty in the White House. Public interest in them was spontaneous, as pictures of Theodore, Edith, and their six children began appearing in newspapers and magazines. For once in history, the executive mansion acquired aspects of a normal American home, complete with roller skates, bicycles, and tennis rackets.

He did lots more after moving into the White House. He even won the Nobel Peace Prize. Not bad for someone who had begun life as a sickly, nearsighted kid with asthma!

EXPLORE!

Across the country, areas large and small are being transformed from pavement to parkland. People are seeing the value of open space, even in the middle of congested cities. Is anything like this happening in your community? Maybe a neighborhood association is cleaning trash from a vacant lot and "greening it up." Your school, library, or newspaper might have information about local reclamation activities. Is anyone protesting the project? Who and why? Do you agree with them?

If you think the project is worthwhile, see if you can help. If work is just beginning, offer to take photographs of the site before, during, and after the cleanup is done. Your scrapbook could become part of your community's archives—part of history.

From the time he was a boy, Teddy Roosevelt understood that bringing nature to people would help them appreciate it. In his room, he set up his very own natural-history "museum," displaying specimens of insects, birds, and animals he had collected. He charged adults a one-penny admission, while kids could view it for free if they helped out by feeding his critters. Teddy's museum may have helped some of those kids look at nature in a whole new way. The pictures you take in your community can make a difference, too. They may encourage future generations to preserve your local "green space" by showing how ugly it became when it was neglected.

JONAS SALK

October 28, 1914–June 23, 1995

MEDICAL PIONEER

- **Physician**
- **Researcher**
- **Humanitarian**

DIVE IN!

Jonas Salk: Discoverer of the Polio Vaccine by Carmen Bredeson (Enslow, 1993), 112 pages. *People to Know*

Jonas Salk by Victoria Sherrow (Facts on File, 1993), 134 pages. *Makers of Modern Science*

Believe in what you do. Dr. Jonas Salk did. In fact, he believed so strongly in the quality of his medical research that he was willing to risk his own safety to prove that he was right. His wife and his three sons put their lives and health on the line for him, too. A researcher doesn't usually test his own findings, especially on himself and his family. But Dr. Jonas Salk did.

Polio, the short name for poliomyelitis, was a dreaded childhood disease. If you got it, it either killed you or left your body crippled. Most victims contracted the disease in infancy, which is why it was also known as infantile paralysis. Could a cure be found to stop this disease? Did people believe they would ever be free from the danger of polio? Dr. Jonas Salk did.

He worked sixteen hours a day, seven days a week for years to find a way to prevent the disease from attacking kids. Finally, he created a vaccine to immunize people against polio. After successful tests on laboratory animals, it had to be tested on human beings. Who would take the risk? Dr. Jonas Salk did.

Why did the tests involve risks? Because the vaccine consisted of the actual poliovirus. That's right, to prevent the disease from occurring, the disease was actually injected into your body. Pretty scary thought. The killed poliovirus cells in the vaccine built up natural antibodies (fighting cells), in the body. Did people believe the new vaccine would work? Dr. Jonas Salk did.

In 1955, Dr. Jonas Salk became a national hero overnight. Many thought he would win the Nobel Prize in medicine, but he did not. However, President Dwight D. Eisenhower invited Salk and his family to the White House, where he was given a citation.

"The reward for work well done is the opportunity to do more."

—Dr. Jonas Salk

Because they trusted him, Dr. Salk's wife and children also volunteered to be "human guinea pigs." The tests were successful in that they showed the vaccine was not dangerous: None of the people injected with the vaccine got polio. This allowed the vaccine to be tested on a larger scale, eventually proving itself to prevent polio. It was *the* major breakthrough in the 1950s and was the beginning of the end of polio's terrible effects. It was clear to everyone what Jonas Salk had done.

A grateful nation and world applauded his achievement. He could have become a very wealthy man from his discovery, but when asked who would control the polio vaccine, he replied, "There is no patent. Could you patent the sun?" No, such beneficial work should be freely shared—and that's what Dr. Jonas Salk had done.

EXPLORE!

Although Dr. Salk died several years ago, medical research continues at the **Salk Institute for Biological Studies**. To find out what its latest research efforts are, you can write the institute at PO Box 85800, San Diego, CA 92186-5800 or check the Internet at: www.salk.edu. By doing so, you can check out

the institute's research on AIDS, Alzheimer's disease, birth defects, the brain, cancer, gene therapy, hormones, multiple sclerosis, and more.

Dr. Salk himself, even at the age of eighty, was actively involved in research to find a cure for AIDS or a vaccine to prevent its spread. What do you know about AIDS? What do you know about other infectious diseases, like the flu, pneumonia, or even the common cold? As an American, you have access to incredible medical services. Some people say that we have the best doctors and health-care facilities in the world. The cost of all these services has become very high. You can be part of an effort to keep our health system top rate by learning ways to stay healthy. Do you know the right kinds of foods to eat? Do you know the importance of daily exercise? Do you know how you can reduce the chance of getting a disease like AIDS?

A group of schoolchildren wait in line for Dr. Salk's vaccination. These first children who were vaccinated became known as "polio pioneers."

99

TECUMSEH

c. (circa) March 1768—October 5, 1813

"SHOOTING STAR"

- **Statesman**
- **Warrior**

DIVE IN!

The Importance of Tecumseh by Myra H. and William H. Immell (Lucent Books, 1997), 112 pages. Illustrated. *The Importance of*

Tecumseh and the Shawnee Confederacy by Rebecca Stetoff (Facts on File, 1998), 138 pages. *Library of American Indian History*

If you have studied our country's history carefully, you know that before our Constitution was adopted in 1787, we were governed by a document called the Articles of Confederation.

"Confederation" means a joining together for a common purpose. The newly independent American colonies joined together as states in a confederation. Their unity gave them strength.

That's exactly what Tecumseh tried to do with numerous Native American tribes. White people were sweeping across the country, taking land from Native Americans and offering little or no compensation. Tecumseh worked hard to unite the Indians into a strong Shawnee Confederation that could resist this invasion. But it wasn't easy. The members of each tribe were fiercely proud of their individual tribal identities and leaderships.

Tecumseh was a gifted speaker. His words convinced Native Americans that unity would help them hold on to their land. Traveling thousands of miles through the territory east of the Mississippi River, Tecumseh forged the largest united group of Native American nations ever. In 1808 he and his brother, Tenskwatawa, called the Prophet, established a village called Prophetstown. There, confederation members could follow traditional Native American ways and train to defend their land.

Despite its unity, however, the confederation was still unable to halt the westward movement of white settlers. In 1811, Tecumseh's brother sent the unified warriors into battle against white soldiers, although Tecumseh warned that the confederation was not yet strong enough. The warriors were defeated. Prophetstown was destroyed. The Native Americans were scattered.

Like the shooting star that streaked across the sky the night Tecumseh was born, the Shawnee Confederation shone brightly, brilliantly, for a moment. Then it was gone. But just as the image of that shooting star loomed large in the memories

Tecumseh is shown here with General William Henry Harrison, who would later become the ninth president of the United States. Harrison badly defeated the unified Indian groups led by Tecumseh and his brother at the Battle of Tippecanoe.

"Sell a country! Why not sell the air, the clouds, and the great sea as well as the earth? Did not the Great Spirit make them all for the use of his children?"
—Tecumseh

of those who saw it, so does Tecumseh's legacy as a man of influence live on. Respect for him extends far beyond the Native American community. Throughout our country, you will find towns, schools, even a navy submarine named in his honor. He is a hero every kid should meet.

EXPLORE!

Too much of our history was a violent struggle for the control of land—between the Native Americans and those who came to this continent from other areas of the world. In most cases, compromises were rejected, and the solution was an "all or nothing" one. Usually, the Native Americans were the losers.

Tecumseh's story of loyalty to his people and devotion to his land is only one of countless Native American efforts to hold on to their heritage. As a country, we are finally honoring the cultures and contributions of Native Americans. Scheduled to open in 2002, the National Museum of the American Indian will be located on the famous Mall in our nation's capital. There, great Native American leaders like Tecumseh, Chief Joseph, Crazy Horse, Sitting Bull, and so many others will have their stories told, and cultural artifacts from the Cherokee, Shawnee, Sioux, Hopi, and many other tribes and nations will be displayed. Visitors will witness and participate in ceremonies, performances, and educational activities celebrating Native American heritage.

You can learn about this new museum by writing to:

**National Museum of
the American Indian**
Executive Offices
470 L'Enfant Plaza, SW
Suite 7102
Washington, DC 20560

Check the Internet as well.

Maybe you have some ideas about what should be a part of this museum. What would interest you? What do you want to learn about Native Americans? We hope you'll use your school and local libraries to dig in.

EXPLORE SOME MORE!

In a growing number of areas around our country, Native American festivals are being held. Some of these are called powwows. Maybe you can convince your family or friends or a group you belong to, like the Scouts, to attend a festival.

HARRY S TRUMAN

May 8, 1884–December 26, 1972

"GIVE 'EM HELL, HARRY"

- **U.S. President**

- "The buck stops here."
- "Always do right. This will gratify some people and astonish the rest." (Mark Twain)
- "If you can't stand the heat, get out of the kitchen."

These are three of Harry Truman's favorite sayings. In fact, the first two were printed on placards that he kept on his desk. And they weren't just empty slogans. These words guided Truman as he made tough decisions for our country during and after World War II, the most devastating global war in the history of the human race.

During that war, the United States, supposedly the guardian of democracy, had

DIVE IN!

Harry S Truman by Michael A. Schuman (Enslow Publishers, 1997), 112 pages.

The Truman Way by Jeffrey Brandon Morris (Lerner, 1994), 128 pages.

separate army companies for black soldiers and white soldiers. That's right. African-Americans who served in either the Army or Navy were kept apart from white soldiers and sailors. Though they loyally defended America against Nazi Germany and imperial Japan in World War II, black servicemen and servicewomen were treated as second-class citizens in the country for which they had risked their lives.

Harry Truman knew it was wrong to segregate blacks from whites in the military. So, too, did previous presidents, but they chose not to deal with the problem. Not Harry Truman. It was wrong, and he had to change it. The Declaration of Independence said that all people are created equal and should have equal rights. It was that simple. End of discussion. So, in 1948, Harry Truman issued an executive order integrating the United States Armed Services.

Think of what that decision meant. Both black and white sailors would serve on the same ships.

Truman is shown with British Prime Minister Winston Churchill (left) during the Potsdam Conference in 1945 in Germany.

Every public-opinion poll predicted that Republican presidential candidate Thomas Dewey would win a landslide victory in 1948, and some newspapers actually reported Dewey's victory. But through hard campaigning, Truman pulled off one of the biggest upsets in political history, winning 28 states to Dewey's 16.

Black and white soldiers would march side by side. Black Americans could train to be pilots.

Nearly every admiral and general as well as his civilian advisors on military matters tried to talk Truman out of this. But he was the president, the commander in chief. He knew it was the right thing to do ("Always do right . . ."). He made the tough decisions (the "buck" stopped with him). He wasn't afraid of the heat.

Some historians say that Harry Truman made more tough decisions than any other modern president did. Some of the decisions didn't solve the problems, but most of them did. And no one, friend or foe, can ever accuse him of not doing his job.

EXPLORE!

Harry S Truman was guided by the slogans he kept on his desk. Every day they reminded him of how he wanted to conduct himself. "The buck stops here" meant he accepted responsibility. Do you? When you make a mistake, do you own up to it or do you try to "pass the buck"?

Find at least two slogans from famous quotes that can help you become a more responsible individual. Where do you look? Try:

Scholastic Treasury of Quotations for Children by Adrienne Betz (Scholastic Trade, 1998)

Quotations for Kids by Joyce Senn (Millbrook, 1999)

Quotes for Kids: Today's Interpretations of Timeless Quotes Designed to Nurture the Young Spirit by Lisa Meyer (Reach Press, 1998)

Kids Book of Wisdom: Quotes from the African-American Tradition by Cheryl Willis Hudson and Wade Hudson (Just Us Books, 1997)

Bartlett's Familiar Quotations by John Bartlett, edited by Justin Kaplan (Little, Brown and Co., 1992)

Harry Truman had his slogans right in front of him, so you do the same. Once you've found some quotations that speak to you, print one on a poster or a bookmark. Hang some in your room. Stick one on your mirror, so you'll see it all the time. And just like Truman, put Mark Twain's words about always doing right in a prominent spot, too.

By the way, Harry Truman's middle initial is not followed by a period on purpose. What does it stand for? Do a little digging at the library or on the Internet to find out!

POWER WORDS

"The Bill of Rights applies to everybody in this country, and don't you ever forget it."
—Harry S Truman

HARRIET TUBMAN

c. (circa) 1819 or 1820–March 10, 1913

"MOSES"

- **Abolitionist**
- **Freedom Fighter**

The Promised Land. In Bible stories, it's the place of safety and freedom where the people of Israel were headed, led by a man named Moses. In the 1800s the people seeking safety and freedom were American slaves. The "Promised Land" was the northern part of our country, where slavery was against the law. And Harriet Tubman was "Moses." And, if Harriet Tubman were leading you from slavery to freedom, you'd better not change your mind.

Escaping from slavery was incredibly dangerous for both the escapees and for those helping them escape. Slaves were considered the property of their owners. Helping a slave run away was like stealing a slaveholder's stuff. Recaptured slaves were in big trouble. Owners would haul them back, beat them, and make their lives even more miserable than before. Harriet Tubman managed to escape from slavery, but she didn't settle into a quiet life of freedom. Instead, she kept going back to lead others to the Promised Land. Three hundred others, altogether. She led them to a series of safe houses, where people lived who would help runaway slaves find freedom. This network of hiding places was called the Underground Railroad. Harriet was one of the Railroad's courageous "conductors."

Once a slave decided to hop on the Railroad, there was no turning back. Harriet Tubman made sure of that. When somebody got too scared to go on, Harriet would sometimes "encourage" the person by pointing a gun at his or her head! She knew that going to the Promised Land was risky. But going back to slavery was worse.

Angry slaveholders hated Harriet. They offered a huge reward for her capture. Everyone was looking for her. But this conductor of the Underground Railroad was never caught. And neither was any slave she led to freedom.

DIVE IN!

Harriet Tubman: Conductor of the Underground Railroad by Ann Petry (HarperTrophy, 1996), 64 pages.

Harriet and the Promised Land by Jacob Lawrence (Simon & Schuster, 1993), 32 pages.

"On my Underground Railroad, I never ran my train off the track, and I never lost a passenger."
— Harriet Tubman

EXPLORE!

Thousands of runaway slaves owed their lives and their liberty to the Underground Railroad. The huge network of safe places leading to freedom was maintained by hundreds of brave people who saw slavery for what it was: a vicious evil that had to be abolished.

Lots of books and articles have been written about the Underground Railroad, but there's been no way of tracing all the routes and identifying the Railroad "stations" as they are today. But all that is changing. The U.S. National Park Service has conducted a study to figure out the best way to preserve and remember the Underground Railroad. The sheer size of the Railroad makes this an awesome task. We're talking about thousands of miles of roads and paths through almost three dozen states and parts of Canada. There were also hundreds of safe houses, and some of them are gone now.

Find out more about this gigantic project by contacting the National Park Service (www.nps.gov/undergroundrr). Find out if the Underground Railroad passed through your community. If it did, maybe you can get involved in the preservation effort.

Another contact is the

National Underground Railroad Freedom Center
312 Elm Street, 20th Floor
Cincinnati, OH 45202
Phone: (888) 684-7732
On the Web: www.underground railroad.com

This educational museum center is set to open in 2003. It will celebrate the courage of the runaway slaves and the people who helped them. The goal? To promote understanding, healing, and reconciliation.

Harriet Tubman, a runaway slave herself, returned to the South nineteen times and helped about three hundred blacks escape to freedom. She is shown here (at far left) with some of the people she led out of slavery.

GEORGE WASHINGTON

February 22, 1732–December 14, 1799

"FATHER OF OUR COUNTRY"

- **U.S. President**
- **Commander in Chief**

Every country in the 1700s had kings or queens or emperors. Young George Washington was a loyal subject of the king of England. He was proud to be English and eager to serve his king and country. He had risked his life defending English rule in the colonies in the French and Indian War. But the king and his advisors mistreated the American colonies until the colonists finally said "Enough!" The Revolutionary War followed, and in 1776 the United States of America became an independent nation. George Washington led America's troops to victory over the British.

During the war for independence, a group of officers pleaded with Washington to declare himself "king." But the general told them that they were fighting for freedom and a new form of self-government. It made no sense to trade one King George (III) for a new King George! After the war he retired as a true war hero to his Mount Vernon, Virginia, plantation. There he watched the new nation take shape.

With the acceptance of the Constitution in 1788, all eyes turned to the general to lead the new government. Would he accept the newly created office of "president?" He really wanted to stay at home. He was not seeking political power.

But George Washington was a humble man of strong character and solid virtues—and he believed in democracy. He agreed to be president because he believed that people should choose their leaders, and the people wanted him.

An idealized portrait of Washington as he must have looked in April 1789 when he rode his horse through every city and town from Mount Vernon to New York, where he was inaugurated.

President Washington's leadership and personal charisma shaped our young country as no other person could have done. He was indeed, "first in war, first in peace, and first in the hearts of his countrymen." (Richard Henry Lee, a good friend and fellow soldier, said that about Washington.)

EXPLORE!

To honor the "Father of Our Country," we have used his name in many different places. We wonder how humble George would react to all this fuss! First there's Washington, D.C., capital of our nation and

"The power under the Constitution will always be with the people."
—George Washington

On Christmas Day 1776, General George Washington led his troops in a surprise attack against the British, who had settled into winter quarters in New Jersey. The American forces crossed the Delaware River at night and defeated the British troops, first at Trenton and then at Princeton. These were not major victories, but they served to greatly improve the flagging morale of the American forces.

possibly the most important city in the world. What a wonderful place to visit. And what a great tribute to the great man who helped plan the "Federal City" but never lived there.

How many other places in this country are named for George Washington? Pull out a map of your home state. Any rivers, lakes, or mountains bearing his name? Now look through an atlas of all fifty states and watch your list grow.

Another great tribute to our first president is the world-famous Washington Monument. Did you know that no building in the capital city may be taller than the Washington Monument? Why? This 555-foot-tall obelisk has a fascinating history. Request a brochure from

Washington Monument
The National Capital Parks–Central
The National Mall
900 Ohio Drive, SW
Washington, DC 20242
Phone: (202) 426-6841
On the Web: www.nps.gov/wamo/home.htm

And did you know that there's actually a second tower in Washington's honor only five miles from the famous one? Ask for information on the "other Washington Monument":

George Washington Masonic National Memorial
Shooters Hill
101 Callahan Drive
Alexandria, VA 22301
Phone: (703) 683-2007

EXPLORE SOME MORE!

Take a virtual tour of George Washington's Mount Vernon home. Go to: www.mount vernon.org/image/mansiontour. You won't believe how cool this is!

DIVE IN!

George Washington and the Birth of Our Nation by Milton Meltzer (Franklin Watts, 1986), 176 pages.

IDA B. WELLS

July 16, 1862–March 25, 1931

THE ANTI-LYNCHING CRUSADER

- **Journalist**
- **Humanitarian**

Ida B. Wells-Barnett is shown with her family in 1909: Charles (14), Herman (12), Ida (8), and Alfreda (5).

Ida Wells, a twenty-one-year-old school teacher, was literally thrown off the train. She had refused to move to the car reserved for blacks. She sued the railroad company, won the case, but then lost when the railroad company appealed to the Tennessee State Supreme Court. Asked to write an article for a black church's weekly newsletter, she did so—launching her career as a crusading journalist.

Did you ever hear the expression "the pen is mightier than the sword"? Words can be very powerful weapons. Words can stop trouble dead in its tracks. Words can right wrongs and ease another person's anger. Words can change people's minds and even their hearts. That's what Ida B. Wells did with words. She knew the power behind the pen.

Born a slave in Mississippi during the Civil War, Ida was too young to know the power of the words issued on January 1, 1863. But Abraham Lincoln's words on that day, the words in the Emancipation Proclamation, freed baby Ida from slavery. Truly those were powerful words, which later on she would learn and love.

Ida B. Wells was a gifted writer. Her career as a newspaper journalist began as a young woman in her twenties when she began to write letters to some African-American newspapers. She wasn't afraid to tell the truth, which was (and is) a reporter's job. During this post–Civil War time, angry, prejudiced white people in the South began

a fifty-year period of senseless violence against freed African Americans. Lynchings (hangings, shootings, or burnings) were an epidemic. Thousands of innocent blacks were killed by mobs. The country ignored the problem; that is, until Ida B. Wells forced the nation to pay attention.

A friend of Ida B. Wells was lynched. Murdered by a mob. No trial, no justice— just brutal, senseless mob violence. As a black person, she knew that members of her race were more often the victims of lynch mobs than were whites. She gathered evidence to prove her case. Then she presented the facts in a newspaper called *Free Speech*. How powerful were her words? So

"There must always be a remedy for wrong and injustice if we only know how to find it."
—Ida B. Wells

powerful that her life was threatened. Her words had led to successful boycotts in Memphis, Tennessee, her home. When she wrote that blacks should leave the city because they were no longer safe, thousands did so. When she wrote that blacks should stop riding the streetcars, thousands did so. In fact, it's interesting to compare the streetcar boycott she helped promote with the famous bus boycotts of the 1950s and 1960s civil-rights movement.

Ida B. Wells (later known as Wells-Barnett) moved to New York City to stay safe. From there, she continued her war of words against mob rule. Her writings became world famous, and her words helped awaken people's minds and hearts to the tragedy. She truly proved that the pen *was* mightier than the sword.

EXPLORE!

When was the last time you wrote a letter? No, we're not talking about chat room messages or the notes you pass in study hall. We mean a *real* letter, like the ones you see on the opinion page of the newspaper. A letter that tells a story or communicates an idea that you believe is important. A letter that can make a difference.

In the early 1980s, a ten-year-old girl named Samantha Smith wrote a letter to Yuri Andropov, who had just become the leader of the Soviet Union. Samantha told President Andropov that she was worried about the United States and his country getting into a nuclear war. Believe it or not,

President Andropov answered Samantha's letter and invited her to visit the Soviet Union. Their meeting made headlines around the world. Although Samantha's life was cut short when she died in a plane crash in 1985, she proved that the pen is still powerful, even in the hand of a child.

Find out more about Samantha and other exceptional young people at the library or on the Internet. Let them give you confidence in your ability to make a difference. Then sit down and write a letter.

DIVE IN!

Ida B. Wells-Barnett and the Anti-Lynching Crusade by Suzanne Freedman (The Millbrook Press, 1994), 32 pages.

Ida B. Wells-Barnett: Crusader Against Lynching by Elaine Slivinski Lisandrelli (Enslow, 1998), 128 pages.

109

ELIE WIESEL

September 30, 1928–

SURVIVOR OF THE HOLOCAUST

- **Humanitarian**
- **Teacher**
- **Author/Playwright**
- **Recipient, Nobel Peace Prize**

Some really stupid people are saying the Holocaust never happened—but it did. Elie Wiesel knows it happened because he was there and he survived.

Have you ever heard of Auschwitz? It was a terrible place in Poland, one of the "death camps" (also known as concentration camps) where innocent people were slaughtered by the German Nazis during the 1940s. Elie Wiesel was only fifteen years old when he saw Nazi soldiers lead his mother and younger sister to their deaths in an Auschwitz gas chamber. Later, at another death camp called Buchenwald, he watched his father die of hunger and disease.

Following the defeat of the Nazis in 1945 and the world's discovery of the horrors of the death camps, sixteen-year-old Elie was taken to France. Try to imagine how he felt. He was now an orphan. He had witnessed incredible scenes of brutality and torture on a daily basis. He had felt the gut-wrenching

pangs of hunger and had been beaten when camp guards were mad at him. He had worked daily surrounded by fellow Jews who were sick and dying. And he bore a number—A17713—that the Nazis had tattooed on him, so that they could strip him of his name along with his human dignity. So many of the people who had been part of young Elie's life were gone. His parents—gone. His neighbors and friends from his small village of Sighet in Transylvania—gone. His teachers who had praised his schoolwork—gone. And his rabbi, who for his Bar Mitzvah had taught him the Torah—gone. Elie Wiesel's childhood had disappeared!

Life had to begin anew for him. Miraculously, two of his sisters had also survived the death camps, and in France he was reunited with them. Strength came from having family back in his life.

Determination came, too, as he realized that he could not remain silent about what he had witnessed. He had vowed to say nothing for ten years. It was too painful to discuss what he had seen. But as reporters and historians started to reveal the magnitude of the death camp horrors, Elie Wiesel began to see his life's mission. More than six million blameless people, most of them Jewish and more than one and a half million of them children, were murdered in those death camps. Wiesel had lived through

This army file photo taken at Buchenwald concentration camp on April 16, 1945, is a rare visual documentation of the inhuman treatment of camp inmates during the Holocaust. Elie Wiesel is the man whose face can be seen at the far right of the center bunk.

that horrible nightmare, that "hell on Earth." He knew that the world had to learn about and remember what had taken place there. And so he began to write and lecture about his experience as a survivor.

Through his work, Elie Wiesel became the voice for the Holocaust. That's what he called the mass murder by the Nazis, and it is the label the world now uses to identify that horrendous ordeal. In the Greek language, the word holocaust means, "a sacrifice burned in its entirety." Those six million men, women, and children were all sacrificed, and Elie Wiesel wanted to prevent it from ever happening again.

In 1963 he became an American citizen, having moved to New York City to continue his speaking and writing. It had been American soldiers who nearly twenty years earlier had set him free.

DIVE IN!

Elie Wiesel: Voice From the Holocaust by Michael Schuman (Enslow Publishers, 1994), 128 pages. *People to Know*

Spared a torturous death in his youth, Elie Wiesel has worked hard to promote world peace and human rights. His more than three dozen books have made him a world-famous author. In 1986, Wiesel received the Nobel Peace Prize in recognition of his efforts to make our world a safer, more loving place. He used his prize money of $290,000 to establish **The Elie Wiesel Foundation for Humanity**, an organization that promotes the elimination of hate and intolerance. Today he serves as a professor at Boston University. His voice for human rights and peace is stronger than ever.

EXPLORE!

The **United States Holocaust Memorial Museum** opened in 1993 to honor the Holocaust's victims. The museum was built to help us remember, learn, and keep this from happening again. Read Elie Wiesel's Power Words. Can we afford to forget the Holocaust? If we do, who will be the next victims? Your neighbor? Your teacher? Your family? You? We must remember. Contact the

**United States Holocaust
Memorial Museum**
100 Raoul Wallenberg Place SW
Washington, DC 20024
On the Web: www.ushmm.org
(E-mail: education@ushmm.org)

Plan to visit this museum someday, too. Remember . . . and learn.

WILBUR AND ORVILLE WRIGHT

Wilbur: April 16, 1867–May 30, 1912

Orville: August 19, 1871–January 30, 1948

THE FIRST MEN TO FLY

- **Inventors**
- **Aviators**

An interesting double portrait of the Wright brothers in profile. Orville is in the foreground.

Count 1001, 1002, 1003, 1004, 1005, 1006, 1007, 1008, 1009, 1010, 1011, 1012. That's twelve seconds. That's how long the historic first airplane flight lasted. Just twelve seconds. The plane flew 120 feet, not even half a football field. But it was enough to prove that humans could fly. Two brothers, Orville and Wilbur Wright, designed and built the motor-driven machine that picked them up off the ground on December 17, 1903, and sent them soaring into the history books. What led the Wright brothers to that historic event on the beach at Kitty Hawk, North Carolina? Well, believe it or not, it was a bicycle.

Ten years earlier, Wilbur and Orville had opened a bicycle repair shop in Ohio. They then began designing new bicycles. Their success in building lightweight bikes, combined with their fascination with glider pilots like Otto Lilienthal, led them to a new interest: flying.

When they were children, their father surprised them once with a toy helicopter. It was made of cork, bamboo,

POWER WORDS

"I cannot but believe that we stand at the beginning of a new era, The Age of Flight."
—Orville Wright

and paper, and powered by a rubber band. They loved playing with it, and used it as a model to make their own. Years later, Wilbur and Orville claimed that their toy helicopter contributed to their interest in flying. Their first experiments with flight involved nonpowered machines called gliders.

They spent years learning the principles of flight before they moved on to powered aircraft. Then there were more years of study and experimentation, until Orville piloted that historic twelve-second

The Wright brothers prepare one of the earlier versions of their plane for take-off. It was not only their knowledge of aerodynamics but also their skill as pilots that contributed to their eventual success.

flight, with Wilbur running alongside the airplane. Three more flights took place that morning, with the brothers taking turns at the controls. The longest flight of the day was 852 feet and lasted 59 seconds. Wilbur was in the pilot's seat.

Then Wilbur and Orville became rich and famous, right? Wrong! The world didn't even hear about what they'd done for another five years. Want to know why? You'll have to read their story to find out!

EXPLORE!

In the year 2003, we'll commemorate the one hundredth anniversary of the Wright brothers' first flight. So how should we celebrate this monumental birthday? We want your ideas.

First, you might want to learn more about flying and aviators. Contact:

The National Air and Space Museum
6th Street and
Independence Avenue, SW
Washington, DC 20560
On the Web: http://www.nasm.edu/ NASMhome.html
E-mail: mtuttle@ceps.nasam.edu

DIVE IN!

The Wright Brothers: How They Invented the Airplane by Russell Freedman (Holiday House, 1991), 128 pages. 1992 Newbery Honor Book

The Wright Brothers National Memorial
c/o Cape Hatteras National Seashore
Route 1, Box 675
Manteo, NC 27954

Greenfield Village
20900 Oakwood Boulevard
PO Box 1970
Dearborn, MI 48121-1970
Phone (313) 982-6001 or
(800) 835-5237
On the Web: www.hfmgv.org

Pump up your research with a blast of imagination and decide how we should celebrate the centennial of flight. Write or E-mail us with your clever ideas. We'll collect them and submit them *on your behalf* to the people who plan the centennial. Just think, your idea might actually become part of this national celebration.

We want to challenge *you*! Too often, authors think they have to tell you everything. Well, we know that you can track down even more interesting stories of real heroes on your own if we provide a "trail." So, get your computer ready—or your set of encyclopedias—and start hunting!

All the new heroes you will discover have some connection with one of our 50. Think about the links, and figure out how you might even become connected if a particular hero piques your curiosity.

It's not a contest, but we would love to know how many heroes you found before you turned to the answers on page 127. E-mail us at the Web site found in this book's introduction.

HAPPY HUNTING!

1. **(Jane Addams, p. 14)** Just as Miss Addams was crusading to help the poor, another courageous woman was raising her voice to help the mentally ill. At one time, people who were mentally ill received time in jail instead of medical care. This woman fought, and won; major changes followed. Who is she?

2. **(Susan B. Anthony, p. 16)** Susan B. is sort of the MVP of the All-Star team of Suffragettes. You'll learn about some of the other team members from the information you receive from Seneca Falls—people like Elizabeth Cady Stanton and Lucretia Mott. But there's an earlier champion of women's rights in our country. During the founding days of our new nation, she continually reminded her husband of the importance of equal rights for women. He listened, but didn't break from the traditions of the times. Who is this woman? Hint: she became our second First Lady.

3. **(Clara Barton, p. 18)** Congress recently named this modern-day "angel" of a very different battlefield an honorary American citizen. Her "battlefields" were city slums in India, where she and her "sisters" provided care for the poorest of the poor. Who is this remarkable person?

4. **(Elizabeth Blackwell, p. 22)** This accomplished African-American surgeon also knew what it was like to struggle against prejudice while pursuing a dream. He crusaded for better medical care for black people, counseled and assisted black medical students, encouraged black women to become nurses, and helped found one of the first interracial hospitals in America. Who is he?

5. **(Rachel Carson, p. 24)** We Americans love our cars, and we drive more of them than any nation in the world. But have all of our automobiles always been as safe as they should have been? One

person didn't think so, and he wrote a book called *Unsafe at Any Speed* to get his message out to consumers and car manufacturers. And he was successful. Who is he?

6. **(Jimmy Carter, p. 26)** One of the humanitarian efforts that Jimmy Carter and his family support is building homes for poor people. It's a national effort called Habitat for Humanity. Who is the husband-and-wife team—two of Jimmy's real heroes—who started and continue to run this wonderful organization?

7. **(George Washington Carver, p. 28)** Dr. Carver worked with peanuts, but this famous scientist experimented with corn. Her parents did not want her to attend college, but she found a way to go. Genetics was her specialty. Who is she?

8. **(Bill Cosby, p. 36)** As a child, Bill's loving mother, Anna, often read him the classic books written by one of our country's greatest authors. His stories of mischievous boys like Tom and Huck helped shape Bill's funny stories. Who is the author?

9. **(Walt Disney, p. 38)** This "dreamer's" characters are also a wonderful part of our popular culture. Some of you learned to count and to read with their help when you visited their "Street." And surely all of us know about the romance between a certain pig and a frog! Who is this heroic artist?

10. **(John Glenn, p. 48)** He never flew in outer space. Yet he's called "The Father of the U.S. Space Program." He was the guiding force behind our efforts to explore the new frontier. His work with rockets, beginning in the 1920s, paved the way for men walking on the moon. Who is he?

11. **(Milton Hershey, p. 54)** This woman was also a successful entrepreneur, who invented special hair-care products for African-American women. In 1918 she became the first African-American woman to become a millionaire. Although she lived quite comfortably, she also donated a great deal of money to the NAACP, the YMCA, a school in West Africa, and to educational funds to help women and African Americans. Who is she?

12. **(Helen Keller and Anne Sullivan, p. 60)** A very famous inventor was a good friend of Helen's parents. This man recommended Annie Sullivan as the teacher who could help young Helen. All his life he hoped his inventions would benefit people with hearing problems. Who is he?

13. **(Jackie Joyner Kersee, p. 62)** As a child, her legs were crippled by the terrible disease known as polio. But by the age of eight she had learned how to walk. Then she learned to run. She was the first American woman to win three Olympic gold medals in running events. Who is she?

14. **(Robert E. Lee, p. 66)** This present-day general was the first African American to serve as Chairman of the Joint Chiefs of Staff, the highest military post in the United States. However, this man is known not only for his military expertise but also for his strong convictions and his leadership of the volunteer movement in America as well. Who is he?

15. **(John Muir, p. 76)** Many kids think he wasn't real. You've probably read folktales about the man who traveled around many parts of the eastern United States planting apple trees. Wearing his cooking pot as his hat, Johnny Appleseed became a familiar sight to frontier settlers. Read about one of our first conservationists and answer this question: What was his real name?

16. **(I. M. Pei, p. 82)** Another Asian American designed a very special monument found in our nation's capital. The simple "Wall" has the names of all Americans

killed in the Vietnam War. Who designed this beloved memorial?

17. **(Christopher Reeve, p. 84)** Although a 1967 diving accident left her without the use of her legs or hands, this woman is an author, artist, and advocate for the disabled. During her term on the National Council on Disability, the Americans with Disabilities Act became law. She is the only person to receive an honorary doctorate from Columbia University. Who is she?

18. **(Roy Rogers and Dale Evans, p. 90)** Roy and Dale weren't the only Western stars popular in America. Another famous "cowboy" actually had Native American roots. He was an expert at doing rope tricks and at making people laugh with his comments on life, his country, and the way people treat each other. Even the world's leaders paid attention when he spoke. Generous and truthful, he once said, "I never met a man I didn't like." When he was killed in a plane crash, the nation mourned. Who is he?

19. **(Theodore Roosevelt, p. 96)** TR's face is one of four on the largest sculpture in America. Who are the three other presidents on the sculpture, what is its name, where is it located, and who is the brilliant artist who created it? (We hope all of you have a chance to see it in person someday. It's really amazing!)

20. **(Jonas Salk, p. 98)** About one hundred years ago, a terrible disease called yellow fever killed many people. A famous medical researcher dedicated his life to finding its cause, and did so. A major research hospital in our nation's capital is named in his honor. Who is he?

21. **(Tecumseh, p. 100)** Almost none of the Native American nations had a written language. Their culture used only the spoken word. Even the "Power Words" quoted above were recorded by an English-speaking listener. One brilliant Cherokee, with the help of his equally intelligent daughter, developed an alphabet for his nation. Who is this father-daughter team?

22. **(Ida B. Wells, p. 108)** Talk about the power of words! This colonial patriot's words made such "common sense" to the people in the American colonists that they wanted to be independent. Before he wrote his famous pamphlet, many colonies wanted to remain Englishmen. After they read his words, many in 1775 wanted to become independent Americans. Who is he?

23. **(Elie Weisel, p. 110)** He personally saved over 50,000 people from being killed during the Holocaust. He wasn't an American citizen, but Congress believed he was so special that they made him an Honorary American (one of only five people in history so honored). Note the address of the Holocaust Museum.

24. **(Wright Brothers, p. 112)** The story of aviation is full of fascinating and courageous heroes. Among them are Charles Lindbergh and Amelia Earhart, whose solo flights earned them a place in history. (What do you mean you never heard of them? Well go look them up!) Anyway, the famous aviator we have in mind is still flying. This person became the first to break the sound barrier. Today, lots of jets fly faster than the speed of sound, but this pioneering pilot was the first to push his plane into sonic boom territory. Who is he?

QUOTATION SOURCES

JANE ADDAMS

Power Words—"Political Reform" in *Democracy and Social Ethics* by Jane Addams, 1902.

SUSAN B. ANTHONY

Power Words—Speech: "Woman's Rights to the Suffrage," 1873, Rochester, NY.

CLARA BARTON

Power Words—Letter to Annie Childs, May 28, 1863, found in *The Life of Clara Barton* by William Barton, vol. I, AMS Press, 1969, reprinted from 1922. Entire text of letter: pp. 221–224.

MARY McLEOD BETHUNE

Power Words—"My Last Will and Testament" by Mary McLeod Bethune, originally published in *Ebony*, August 1955.

ELIZABETH BLACKWELL

Power Words—"Medicine as a Profession for Women" by Elizabeth Blackwell with Emily Blackwell, 1860.

JIMMY CARTER

Power Words—*American Heroes: Their Lives, Their Values, Their Beliefs* by Robert B. Pamplin Jr. and Gary K. Eisler (Master Media Ltd., 1995), page 13. Based on a first-person interview.

GEORGE WASHINGTON CARVER

Story of Carver talking to God—*George Washington Carver: An American Biography* by Rackham Holt (Doubleday, Doran and Co., 1963), pp. 226–227.
FDR quote regarding Carver—Letter from FDR to Dr. Frederick Douglas Patterson, Tuskegee Institute, January 6, 1943.

Power Words—Letter to Booker T. Washington from Carver discussing Carver's appointment to Tuskegee Institute faculty, April 12, 1896.

MARY CASSATT

Power Words—written by Cassatt at age seventy-six. *Cassatt and Her Circle: Selected Letters* edited by Nancy M. Mathews (Abbeville Press, 1984).

CESAR CHAVEZ AND DOLORES HUERTA

Chavez Power Words—Cesar E. Chavez Foundation ("Cesar E. Chavez in His Own Words").
Huerta Power Words—Interview with Dolores Huerta, quoted in *With These Hands: Women Working on the Land* by Joan M. Jensen (The McGraw-Hill Book Co., 1981).

ROBERTO CLEMENTE

Power Words—Speech before the Baseball Writers of Houston, Texas, 1971.

BILL COSBY

Power Words—Statement to the media on January 15, 1997, following his son's tragic death. Also, title of *Time* magazine article, January 27, 1997.

WALT DISNEY

Power Words—Preface to *Walt Disney World* (Walt Disney Company, 1986), page 2.

FREDERICK DOUGLASS

Power Words—Speech at civil-rights mass meeting, Washington, D.C., October 22, 1883.

THOMAS EDISON

Power Words—Said circa 1903, quoted in *Harper's Monthly Magazine*, September 1932.

ALBERT EINSTEIN

Power Words—*The Quotable Einstein* collected and edited by Alice Calaprice (Princeton University Press, 1996), page 223 (quote attributed to Einstein).

BENJAMIN FRANKLIN

Power Words—In a letter to B. Vaughan, March 14, 1743.

JOHN GLENN

Power Words—Address to joint session of U.S. Congress, February 26, 1962.
Power Words—*John Glenn: A Memoir* by John Glenn with Nick Taylor (Bantam Books, 1999), page 404.

MARTHA GRAHAM

Power Words—*Frontiers of Dance: The Life of Martha Graham* by Terry Walter (Thomas Y. Crowell, 1975), page 42. Author was personal friend of Graham.

MATTHEW HENSON

Power Words—from *To the Top of the World: The Story of Peary and Henson* by Pauline K. Angell (Rand McNally, 1964), page 274.

MILTON HERSHEY

Power Words—*An Intimate Story of Milton S. Hershey* by Joseph Richard Snavely (J. Horace McFarland Co., 1957).

LANGSTON HUGHES

Power Words—from *The Dream Keeper and Other Poems*, 1932.

HELEN KELLER

Power Words—*The Story of My Life*, 1902, Chapter 4.

JACKIE JOYNER-KERSEE

Power Words—*American Heroes: Their Lives, Their Values, Their Beliefs* by Robert B. Pamplin Jr. and Gary K. Eisler (Master Media Ltd., 1995), page 70.

REVEREND DR. MARTIN LUTHER KING JR.

Power Words—referenced in body of text.

ROBERT E. LEE

Power Words—referenced in body of text.

LEWIS, CLARK, AND SACAGAWEA

Power Words—The Corps of Discovery, 1805.

YO-YO MA

Power Words—from an interview "Yo-Yo Ma: Inspired by Bach," *Nine Magazine*, Web site: www.kcts.org/whatson/magazine

GEORGE C. MARSHALL

Power Words—Lecture, Oslo University, January 1, 1954.

JOHN MUIR

Power Words—quoted by John T. Nicholas in *National History* magazine, November 1992.

SANDRA DAY O'CONNOR

Power Words—from *Equal Justice: A Biography of Sandra Day O'Connor* by Harold and Geraldine Woods (Dillon Press, 1985).

ROSA PARKS

Power Words—from *I Am Rosa Parks* by Rosa Parks with Jim Haskins (Dial Books for Young Readers, 1997), page 28.

I. M. PEI

Power Words—from an interview "I. M. Pei—Finding Roots," *Harvard Asia Pacific Review*, Web site: www.hes.harvard.educ/ ~hapr/pei

CHRISTOPHER REEVE

"I think a hero . . ." *Still Me* by Christopher Reeve (Ballantine Books, 1998).
Power Words—interview with Oprah Winfrey, May 4, 1998, ABC-TV.

CAL RIPKEN JR.

Power Words—*The Only Way I Know* by Cal Ripken Jr. and Mike Bryan (Penguin Books, 1997).

JACKIE ROBINSON AND BRANCH RICKEY

Power Words—*I Never Had It Made: An Autobiography* by Jackie Robinson as told to Alfred Duckett (The Ecco Press, 1995).

Power Words—"Rickey Should Be Remembered" by Bob Nightengale, April 2, 1997, Web site: www.sportingnews.com

ROY ROGERS AND DALE EVANS

Power Words—*Happy Trails, Our Life Story* by Roy Rogers and Dale Evans with Jane and Michael Stern (Simon and Schuster, 1995), page 206.

ELEANOR ROOSEVELT

Power Words—quoted in *Catholic Digest*, August, 1960, page 102.

FRANKLIN ROOSEVELT

Power Words—First Inaugural Address, March 4, 1933—*Public Papers* vol. 2, 1938, page 11.

THEODORE ROOSEVELT

Power Words—from a speech given in the Dakota Territory, July 4, 1886.

JONAS SALK

Power Words—spoke these words while accepting a special citation from President Dwight Eisenhower at the White House, April 22, 1955.

TECUMSEH

Power Words—Council at Vincennes, Indiana Territory, August 14, 1810. Tecumseh was responding to a request that he sit at "his father's" (Governor William Henry Harrison's) side.

HARRY S TRUMAN

Power Words—from *Plain Speaking: An Oral Biography of Harry S Truman* by Merle Miller (Berkley Publishing Corp., 1973).

HARRIET TUBMAN

Power Words—Words are carved into a plaque hanging in the Cayuga County (New York) Courthouse. Photograph of plaque is found in *Freedom Train* by Dorothy Sterling (Doubleday & Co. Inc., 1954).

GEORGE WASHINGTON

Power Words—from a letter to Bushrod Washington, November 10, 1787.

IDA B. WELLS

Power Words—quote by Ida B. Wells in 1900. Found in *Crusade for Justice* edited by Alfreda M. Duster, 1970.

ELIE WIESEL

Power Words—from Wiesel's acceptance speech, Nobel Peace Prize, Oslo, Norway, December 10, 1986.

WRIGHT BROTHERS

Power Words—from *Miracle at Kitty Hawk: The Letters of Wilbur and Orville Wright* edited by Fred C. Kelly (Farrar, Straus & Young, 1951).

INDEX

HERO HUNT

Answers

1. Dorothea Dix
2. Abigail Adams
3. Mother Teresa
4. Daniel Hale Williams
5. Ralph Nader
6. Millard & Linda Fuller
7. Barbara McClintock
8. Mark Twain
9. Jim Henson
10. Robert Goddard
11. Madam C.J. Walker
12. Alexander Graham Bell
13. Wilma Rudolph
14. General Colin Powell
15. John Chapman
16. Maya Lin
17. Joni Eareckson Tada
18. Will Rogers
19. Thomas Jefferson, Abraham Lincoln, and George Washington; Mt. Rushmore; South Dakota; sculptor was Gutzon Borghum
20. Dr. Walter Reed
21. Sequoya and Ahyoka
22. Thomas Paine
23. Raoul Wallenberg
24. Chuck Yeager

PHOTO CREDITS

Cover photographs courtesy of Reuters/Joe Giza/ Archive Photos (Cal Ripken, Jr.), Corbis/Bettmann (Martha Graham, Harriet Tubman, Thomas Edison, John Muir, Jackie Joyner-Kersee), National Archives (Robert E. Lee), Underwood & Underwood/Corbis-Bettmann (Eleanor Roosevelt), Reuters/Gary Hershorn/Archive Photos (Christopher Reeve)

Photographs courtesy of Corbis/Bettmann-UPI: pp. 14 (both), 15 (right), 21 (bottom), 27, 32, 33 (top), 34 (both), 35 (bottom), 37 (top right, bottom), 38 (bottom), 39 (both), 46, 48, 49, 50, 51 (top), 53 (top), 56, 57 (top), 60 (bottom), 61, 63 (left), 64, 71 (bottom), 74, 79 (top), 80, 85 (top), 87 (top left), 89 (both), 93 (both), 110, 111; Corbis/Bettmann: pp. 15 (left), 16 (both), 17 (top), 18, 19 (top right, bottom), 22, 28, 29 (right), 41 (bottom), 45 (top right), 47 (bottom), 51 (bottom right), 52, 55 (top), 68, 76, 77 (bottom), 88, 101 (left), 104, 112 (top); Library of Congress: pp. 17 (bottom), 40, 77 (top left), 81 (bottom), 107 (left); U. S. National Park Service, Clara Barton National Historic Site: p. 19 (top left); National Portrait Gallery, Smithsonian Institution/Art Resource, NY: pp. 20, 30 (right), 38 (top), 43 (top), 45 (bottom), 57 (bottom), 59 (left), 66, 96, 97 (top); Mary McLeod Bethune Council House NHS, Washington, D.C.: p. 21 (top); Archives, Warren Hunting Smith Library, Hobart and William Smith Colleges, Geneva, NY: p. 23 (top); The Schlesinger Library, Radcliffe Institute, Harvard University: p. 23 (bottom); Alfred Eisenstaedt/Life Magazine © Time, Inc.: p. 25 (top); North Wind Picture Archives: pp. 25 (bottom), 31 (bottom), 42, 53 (bottom), 58, 67 (bottom), 69 (top), 70, 97 (bottom), 100; Liaison Agency: pp. 26 (top © Jim Moore), 30 (left © Roger Viollet), 72 (© Carol Friedman), 81 (top © Steve Allen), 83 (top © Sheila Nardulli; bottom © Michael Springer), 85 (bottom © Brad Markel), 87 (bottom Jeff Katz); Impact Visuals: pp. 26 (bottom © Marc Pokempner), 33 (bottom left © 1995 David Bacon, bottom right © 1993 Marilyn Humphries), 36 (© Deborah Egan-Chin); Iowa State University Library/Special Collections Department: p. 29 (left); Archive Photos: pp. 31 (top), 37 (top left), 77 (top right), 78 (© Reuters/Gary Hershorn) 84 (© Reuters/Gary Hershorn), 86 (© Reuters/Joe Giza), 98 (© Arnold Sachs/CNP), 99 (top; bottom © Nat Fein), 112 (bottom); Pittsburgh Pirates: p. 35 (top); The Granger Collection, New York: p. 41 (top); Image Select/Art Resource, NY: p. 43 (bottom); AP/Wide World Photos: pp. 44, 62, 69 (bottom), 87 (top right); AIP Emilio Segrè Visual Archives: p. 45 (top left); Hulton Getty/Liaison Agency: pp. 47 (top), 51 (bottom left), 60 (top), 71 (top), 75 (top), 101 (right), 103 (bottom), 107 (right), 113; Hershey Community Archives: pp. 54, 55 (bottom); SEF/Art Resource, NY: p. 59 (right); Corbis/Reuters: pp. 63 (right), 82; MLK Center for Non-Violent Social Change: p. 65 (top); Corbis/MacFadden: p. 65 (bottom); The National Archives: pp. 67 (top), 95 (top), 106; ICM Artists/J. Henry Fair: p. 73 (top); Brian Snyder: p. 73 (bottom); George C. Marshall Foundation: p. 75 (bottom); Joel Benjamin: p. 79 (bottom); Roy Rogers Museum: pp. 90, 91 (both); Underwood & Underwood/Corbis-Bettmann: p. 92; Franklin D. Roosevelt Library: p. 94; © Diane Smook: p. 95 (bottom, Neil Estern, sculptor); U. S. Navy/Harry S. Truman Library: p. 102; SuperStock: p. 103 (top); New York Public Library/Schomburg Center: p. 105 (top); Sophia Smith Collection, Smith College: p. 105 (bottom); Department of Special Collections/University of Chicago Library: pp. 108, 109 (both)